Library of Congress Catalog Card Number 97-062-059
ISBN 0-913423-11-4

This book is dedicated to Renee, Carolyn, Dick, Paul, and Dana

Acknowledgements

We wish to express our sincere appreciation to Norman Hamlin and William Ewen, Sr., for reading this manuscript and for their many valuable suggestions, to C. Spanton Ashdown and John H. Shaum, Jr., for providing information concerning the roles of Eastern steamers during the Second World War, to Drew B. Hains for providing the design and format of this volume, and to Susan V. Ewen, Office Manager of the Steamship Historical Society, whose willing and unstinting assistance has expedited this and many other research projects in American maritime history.

Table of Contents

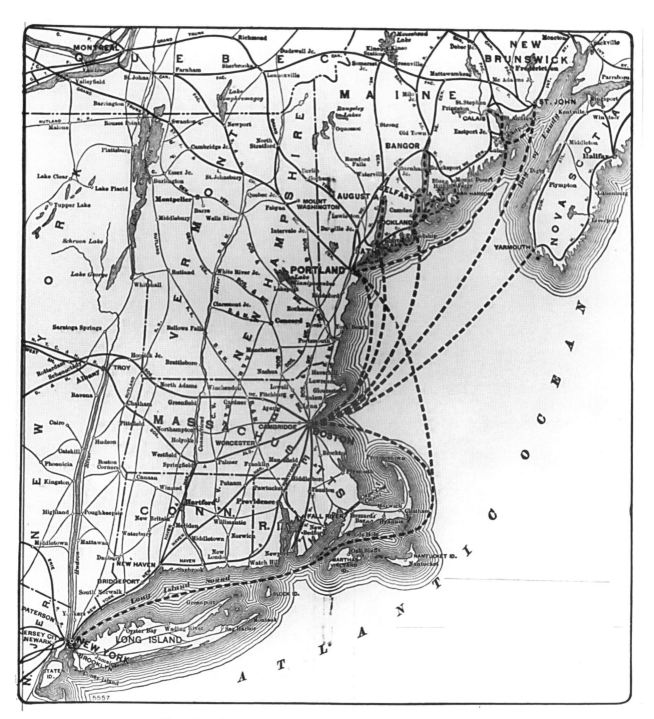

Map showing routes of the Eastern Steamship Company

Introduction

Not least among the casualties of the Second World War were the many steamship lines operating small ocean liners along America's Atlantic coast. In the years before the war literally dozens of coastal liners carried both passengers and cargo on routes such as New York to Boston, New York to Norfolk, or New York to Miami. Some of these routes, like the one from New York to Boston, were merely overnight runs. The New York-to-Miami or New York-to-Havana routes, on the other hand, could include as many as two or three days at sea. In this era before air travel became popular or before the network of federal superhighways rendered long-distance driving somewhat less arduous, many depended on these coastal steamship lines for transportation. These coastal steamship lines also provided opportunities for short inexpensive cruises. In the pre-war years one could enjoy a one-week round trip from Boston or New York to Havana, Nassau or Miami for less than a hundred dollars. For those with less time to spare, a week-end could suffice for an exciting two-day sea trip from New York to Boston or New York to Norfolk, either of which could include tours of colonial sites in the area.

One of the most successful companies operating small ocean liners on routes along the Atlantic Coast was the Eastern Steamship Company. Eastern Steamship was founded early in the century to manage the various overnight steamboat lines between Boston and ports along the coast of Maine. In the 1920s, however, as Eastern began to understand that its short local lines were no longer able to compete with trucks and automobiles, the company began diverting its resources to longer coastal routes in the Atlantic and building the fleet of modern small ocean liners that such routes required.

Until the Second World War summoned all of its its vessels to military duty in 1941, there were often several sailings a day from Eastern's Pier #18 in New York and several more from India Wharf, the company's pier in Boston. Throughout the year, for instance, six days a week one of Eastern Steamship's vessels departed from New York at 11:00 A.M. for Norfolk, Virginia, where she tied up at her wharf at 7:00 the following morning. Another Eastern Steamship vessel pulled out of Pier #18 in New York every day of the year at 5:30 P.M. for an overnight run through Long Island Sound and the Cape Cod Canal to Boston, where she arrived at 8:00 A.M. the next day. On the same schedule a sistership sailed out of Boston every evening for the overnight trip to New York. During the summer months, one of Eastern's newest and largest vessels departed from New York on one round trip per week to Portland, Maine, and one round trip to Yarmouth, Nova Scotia. During the summer season Eastern also scheduled sailings six nights a week in each direction between Boston and Yarmouth and two round trips a week from Boston to St. John, New Brunswick. These were only Eastern Steamship's major routes. Since many of its operations out of New York or Boston were seasonal, Eastern Steamship assigned several of its vessels to relatively short and inexpensive winter cruises out of New York or Boston to Bermuda, Nassau, or one of the inviting island resorts in the Caribbean.

A sailing on one of Eastern Steamship's small ocean liners, even if only an overnight voyage from New York to Norfolk or New York to Boston, could become an event almost as glamorous and exciting as a departure aboard one of the larger liners sailing for Europe. Passengers emerging from a taxi at Eastern's bustling Pier #18 in New York would be greeted by one of the company's porters (men who doubled as Dining Room stewards once the steamer sailed). After gathering up their bags, the porter would guide the arriving passengers down the pier to the gangplank leading up to the ship's large Entrance Hall. Once they had climbed up the gangplank and boarded the waiting steamship, passengers often had the sense of having entered a different world. Aboard ship, the noise, traffic, and dust of the busy city was left behind, and passengers found they had entered the uniquely serene and elegant world of a coastal steamship. Here in the Entrance Hall passengers picked up the keys to their assigned staterooms at the Purser's window. Then the porter would lead them up the wide brass-plated stairway and along a series of carpetted corridors to their staterooms.

Passengers who had paid all of $5.50 for the one-way passage from New York to Boston in the 1930s, $9.00 for a trip from Boston to Yarmouth, or a monumental $12.00 to travel from New York to Norfolk, now laid out anywhere from $1.00 to $10.00 more, depending on the degree of comfort sought, to engage a stateroom. The dollar rooms were small "inside" staterooms with double decker berths. A similar "outside" room could cost fifty cents or a dollar more. A stateroom with beds rather than stacked berths would add a few more dollars to the cost. For ten dollars, the highest price, passengers could relax in a large comfortable room with twin beds and a private bathroom.

As sailing time approached, one of the porters made the rounds of the ship banging on a small gong and shouting "All Ashore Going Ashore!" This call, obviously, was the signal for stateroom farewell parties to end, and for visitors to disembark. Passengers who then climbed up to a higher deck to wave to their friends on the pier might often be startled nearly out of their senses when the steamer's whistle, sometimes only a few yards above them, shrieked its announcement that the ship was about to depart.

For a passenger positioned somewhere forward on an upper deck of a steamship moving slowly out of her pier and heading southward down the Hudson toward the Battery and the Statue of Liberty on her way to Boston, Norfolk, Miami, or Nassau, the excitement at feeling the first rush of cool sea air, the unexpected sense of adventure, could be exhilerating almost beyond comparison. It is surely an experience that cannot be repeated when seated two- or three-abreast on a train, a bus, or an airplane headed for Boston or Norfolk, and certainly not when attempting to navigate an automobile out of the city through crowded holiday traffic.

It is sad to note that one can never again enjoy this unique experience of a short sea trip between two American ports. As a result of the National Emergency declared by President Franklin D. Roosevelt in 1941, even before the bombing of Pearl Harbor had dragged the United States into the most devastating war in history, every one of Eastern Steamship's passenger vessels were requisitioned for war duty. By the time the war ended several of these small liners had been sunk by Nazi submarines. Of those that survived, only two were found to be fit for reconversion to civilian use. With these two vessels Eastern Steamship was able to revive only its Boston-to-Yarmouth service after the war. But times had changed. Tourists in the post-war era often preferred to travel by airplane or in private automobiles, while rapidly rising operating costs soon rendered even the popular Boston-Yarmouth service unprofitable. Finally in 1954, Eastern Steamship sold its two remaining vessels, and the following year the company went out of business.

I. Founding the Eastern Steamship Company: 1901-1905

The Eastern Steamship Company was the creation of one man, Charles Wyman Morse, of Bath, Maine. In Bath, an active seaport and shipbuilding center on the Kennebec River, the Morse family was involved in a variety of local enterprises. As early as 1825, C. W. Morse's grandfather, Wyman Morse, started a towboat line on the Kennebec, which his son, Benjamin Wyman Morse built into the Knickerbocker Towing Company, one of the largest in New England. Benjamin Morse also founded the American Ice Company to collect ice from the pure waters of the upper Kennebec and other Maine rivers each winter, store it in huge warehouses, and transport it to the larger cities farther down the Atlantic Coast when it was needed during the warm summer months. In these days long before the introduction of electric refrigerators or air conditioning, the Maine ice business was an exceptionally profitable enterprise.

Benjamin Morse's son, Charles Wyman Morse, who was born in 1856, was active in his father's ice business even before he graduated from Bowdoin College. In 1880, when he was twenty-four, he moved to New York to manage the ice business at the receiving end. In New York Morse also became involved in local municipal politics. Combining his exceptional business talent with his political connections, and perhaps displaying more than the ordinary indifference to business ethics that was accepted practice in this era, Morse managed by the 1890s to corner and thus control the ice market for the entire city of New York.

Successful and lucrative though this business had become, Morse eventually realized that he had gone as far as he could go with his ice monopoly and decided it was time to try his proven gift for making money in other fields. In 1899 Morse sold his ice company for $12,000,000, a considerable amount of money in this era, and began to look for profitable ways of investing it.

He began by depositing large portions of his $12,000,000 in a few carefully chosen New York banks. The turn of the century was long before American banks had begun amalgamating into mammoth nation-wide conglomerates of which local banks were merely branches. In 1900 there were still many independent banks owned or controlled by a relatively small group of local investors. Morse was astute enough to see that by depositing a few million in one bank and a few million in another, he would be able to place himself in a controlling position in two New York banks and to maintain a considerable influence in others. Then, in any new business ventures, Morse would have at his command not only his own capital but also the assets of the unsuspecting lesser depositors in the banks over which he had acquired influence.

Morse next decided he would like to become involved in the world of coastal steamships. Early in 1901 he returned to Bath to investigate the local steamship operations, and before that year was over Charles W. Morse owned all of the four major overnight steamship lines running out of Boston to ports along the Maine coast.

Morse began locally on the first of April, 1901, by purchasing the Kennebec Steamboat Company from its owners, most of whom were businessmen right in Bath. This line operated the steamers *Kennebec*, built in 1889, and *Sagadahoc*, a much older vessel which had been built in 1866, shortly after the Civil War, as *Star of the East*. This steamer, however, had been rather thoroughly refurbished as well as renamed in 1890 to bring her more or less up to par with the line's newer *Kennebec*. The service of this company called for one of these two steamers to depart from Boston every evening at 6:00 P.M. and steam overnight up the coast to the Kennebec River, where she made stops at the summer resorts and other towns near the mouth of the river in the early morning before proceeding on to Bath and other landings along the way as far as Gardiner, the head of navigation for the larger steamers. At Gardiner passengers could transfer to the small sternwheeler *Della Collins* to venture farther upriver as far as Augusta. The other steamer departed from Gardiner at 3:00 in the afternoon (after the arrival of *Della Collins* from Augusta) and from Bath at 6:00 P.M. to make the overnight run to Boston. The

Kennebec Line, of course, was a seasonal operation, in part because travel to the Maine coast declined considerably during the winter, but more particularly because the Kennebec River tended to be frozen at least during January and February and often well into March.

Single-stacked sidewheelers with big decorated paddle-boxes and wooden hulls so strongly ribbed that they needed no hog frames, *Kennebec* and *Sagadahoc* were typical of the steamboats that had been serving on the Maine coast overnight lines since the 1860s. Their Main Decks, save for the Quarter Deck Entrance Hall and a few staterooms aft of it (usually designated the "Ladies' Cabin," though not necessarily reserved for women travellers), were devoted to side-loaded cargo. The Saloon Deck above had rows of staterooms along both sides. Between the rows of staterooms forward of the stack and walking-beam housing was a dining area. Aft was a lounge furnished with what passed for comfortable chairs and settees in those days, all invitingly upholstered in deep plush. On the Hurricane Deck above stood a Pilot House forward, with a few cabins aft of it for the senior officers. Since traffic had been increasing on the route during the late 1890s, both *Kennebec* and *Sagadahoc* had recently had several extra staterooms added aft on this top deck.

In April 1901, at the same time that he bought the Kennebec Line, Morse also acquired the Eastern Steamboat Company, a line operating a fleet of small day boats from Bath down to Popham Beach, Boothbay Harbor, and other towns or resorts on the islands at the mouth of the Kennebec River. This also was essentially a seasonal operation.

Charles W. Morse had no intention of ending his buying spree after purchasing only the two steamer lines serving his home town. His plan apparently, even in these more modest early days, was to unite all of the steamer services between Boston and ports along the Maine Coast. At the time each of these overnight steamer lines was owned by a relatively small group of investors, some based in Boston but most in the Maine towns at the other end of the routes. Morse believed he was justified in offering top dollar for each of these companies. Once they had been almalgamated, he reasoned, the lines collectively could operate more efficiently and therefore also more profitably than they had as separate companies. The lines could function under a single management team, for instance. Other examples of economy might be com-

Charles Wyman Morse

bining wharf usage and dock crews in Boston, seeking lower insurance rates, shifting steamers from one line to another in response to changing traffic demands, or maintaining only one or two spare steamers for several lines rather than one spare for each route. Also, as Morse understood from his experience in the ice business, the man who controls all of a particular business, with no competitors, can name his own prices either for services rendered or for services sought.

Given these assumptions, Charles W. Morse approached the Boards of Directors of the various Maine coast steamship lines and in each case made an offer, cash on the barrelhead, considerably higher than the figure these people knew to be the assessed value of their marine properties. In each case the response was an enthusiastic agreement to sell. In this manner Morse acquired the Portland Steamship Company (formerly the Portland Steam Packet Company), which ran overnight steamers between Boston and

State of Maine (From the Collection of Frank E. Claes)

Cumberland, which ran with the similar *State of Maine* on the International Line's route from Boston to Portland, Eastport, Lubec, and St. John.

St. Croix ran on the International Line's direct route from Boston to St. John, N.B.

Portland, in May, 1901, the Boston and Bangor Steamship Company (formerly the Sanford Line) in September (and with it a line that connected with the Bangor steamer at Rockland to take passengers and cargo during the day across Penobscot Bay and out to Bar Harbor on Mt. Desert Island), and early in October the International Steamship Company, operating steamers between Boston and St. John, New Brunswick, with stops along the way at Portland, Lubec, and Eastport, Maine. Morse's total outlay in acquiring these four steamship lines was slightly over $1,730,500. While the Kennebec Line, Morse's first acquisition, could not operate in the winter, all of the other lines maintained services throughout the year, although on curtailed schedules in the winter months. In mid-winter, when the Penobscot was frozen, the Bangor boats often had to end their runs at Rockland.

On October 8, 1901, the four overnight steamer lines Morse had acquired, as well as the lines of small day boats both on the Kennebec River and on Penobscot Bay, were brought under a unified management and incorporated in the State of Maine as the Eastern Steamship Company (a name borrowed from the line of small steamers running from Morse's home town out to Boothbay Harbor). Calvin Austin, who had been the managing executive of the Boston and Bangor Line, was installed as President, while Charles Wyman Morse himself served as Chairman of the Board.

With the four overnight steamship lines now forming the Eastern Steamship Company, Morse controlled all but two of the major coastal lines serving the State of Maine. Of the two that had not been gathered into Morse's basket, on one, owned by the Maine Central Railroad, the steamer *Frank Jones* operated out of Portland rather than Boston. From Portland she took an overnight run to Bar Harbor, and from there during the day to landings up the coast as far as Machiasport. The following day *Frank Jones* retraced her route to Bar Harbor and Portland. This line was thoughtful enough to go out of business voluntarily at the end of the 1904 season. The other was the Maine Steamship Company, which operated the ocean-going steel-hulled steamers *Horatio Hall* and *North Star*, and also the smaller wooden-hulled *Manhattan*, between New York and Portland. Needless to say, Morse had a covetous eye trained on the latter, control of which could have connected his Maine steamship

City of Bangor, which ran opposite *City of Rockland* on the route from Boston to Rockland and landings on the Penobscot River as far as Bangor. (From the Collection of Frank E. Claes)

City of Rockland
(R. Loren Graham Collection, Steamship Historical Society, University of Baltimore Library)

Penobscot, the spare steamer of the Boston and Bangor Line.
(Steamship Historical Society Collection, University of Baltimore Library)

operations with the lucrative markets of New York.

In 1902, the year after he had created his Eastern Steamship Company, Charles W. Morse also purchased the two primary overnight lines on the Hudson River: The People's Line, better known as the Albany Night Line, which operated large wooden-hulled sidewheel steamers between New York and Albany, and the Citizens' Line, which ran similar, though smaller, steamers between New York and Troy. These two lines Morse later combined as the Hudson River Navigation Company. Although Morse continued to manage these Hudson River lines for the rest of his life, they remained a separate operation and were never incorporated into his Eastern Steamship Company of Maine.

Of the four steamer lines serving the coast of Maine which comprised Morse's Eastern Steamship Company, the International Line had the longest route with a run of 330 miles in each direction. Three days a week one of its steamers departed from Boston at 8:00 in the morning, put in at Portland late that afternoon, continued up the Maine coast overnight to make early morning landings at both Lubec and Eastport in northeastern Maine (ports famous for their sardine factories and other fish-packing plants), and proceeded during the second day to St. John, New Brunswick. Here the steamer remained overnight before repeating the trip back to Boston. On this route the International Line operated two similar steamers, *State of Maine* (1882) and *Cumberland* (1885). These steamers too were of the typical Maine coast type and resembled the steamers of the Kennebec Line, except that they carried two slightly raked smokestacks athwartship. A third steamer of this line, *St. Croix*, which made a twice-weekly run directly from Boston to St. John and back, was a different type. As a propeller steamer with a narrow black hull without overhanging guards, she resembled a small ocean-going vessel. Although she had been planned in this fashion in order to take on the frequently stormy winter weather off the Maine coast, her design was apparently not entirely successful, for *St. Croix* was known as a roller and was never particularly popular with passengers.

The Boston and Bangor Steamship Company was one of the oldest steamer lines in America, having been in continuous operation since it was founded in 1845 by Menemon Sanford. The steamers of the

The day steamer, *Mount Desert*, which met the Bangor boats at Rockland to take transfer passengers to points around Penobscot Bay and to Bar Harbor.
(R. Loren Graham Collection, Steamship Historical Society, University of Baltimore Library)

234-mile Boston-to-Bangor route plied the second longest run of the Maine Coast lines. Departing from Boston at 5:00 P.M. six nights a week, the Bangor boat sailed overnight up the coast to pull up to the wharf in Rockland, near the entrance to Penobscot Bay, at 5:00 A.M. Here passengers could transfer to one of the smaller steamers waiting with steam up at Tillson's Wharf to ferry them during the day to various destinations around Penobscot Bay. Largest among the day boats was the popular *Mt. Desert*, which Morse had acquired with his purchase of the Boston and Bangor Line. This steamer pulled out of Rockland early every morning, after she had taken aboard the transfer passengers and freight from the Bangor boat, and steamed first to several landings across Penobscot Bay and then out to stops on Mt. Desert Island until she reached Bar Harbor about noon. In the afternoon she retraced this route in time to connect with the outbound Bangor Line steamer at Rockland in the early evening.

After leaving Rockland, the overnight steamer continued up the Penobscot River making several landings along the way until she reached Bangor about 11:00 A.M. Three hours later, she pulled away from her pier at Bangor again, made her way back down

the river to Rockland during the afternoon, and sailed from there that evening (after taking on passengers and freight from the day boats from various points on Penobscot Bay that met her at Rockland) in time to arrive back in Boston at 7:00 A. M. the next morning.

The two primary steamers of the Bangor route, *City of Bangor* (1894) and *City of Rockland* (1901) were both larger (over 275 feet in overall length) and more modern than the steamers of either the Kennebec Line or the International Line. Although these steamers were also wooden-hulled sidewheelers with walking-beam engines, they were the only Maine coast steamers to date to be propelled with the smaller and more efficient feathering sidewheels or to carry two full decks of staterooms for passengers, with an open well between them, in the manner of the larger steamers then operating on Long Island Sound. Built seven years apart, these two steamers had somewhat different outward appearances, but as their stateroom layouts were virtually identical, they were considered sisterships. *City of Bangor* carried two thin stacks athwartship and had a more pronounced sheer, whereas *City of Rockland*, which had just arrived on the line when Morse bought the company in 1901,

Kennebec, which ran opposite the older *Sagadahoc* on the route from Boston to Bath and other landings on the Kennebec River. (Steamship Historical Society Collection, University of Baltimore Library)

had a single neatly raked stack and less sheer. *City of Rockland* was clearly the handsomer vessel, but the older *City of Bangor* was generally considered both faster and more dependable.

Penobscot (1882), the older spare steamer of the Bangor Line, was similar in size and style to the two steamers of the Kennebec Line. Shortly before Morse purchased the company *Penobscot* had been chartered to the Joy Line on Long Island Sound for the summer.

With only a 110-mile run from port to port and no landings to make along the way, the steamers of the Portland Line had the shortest route of the Maine overnight boats. The steamer departing from her Boston wharf at 6:00 P.M. could, without even developing full steam power, tie up at her dock in Portland by 4:30 the following morning. Nevertheless, the Portland boats carried more passengers and considerably more cargo than the steamers of the other Maine coast lines. Portland was not only the major commercial center of Maine, it was also a railroad hub with rail lines extending to other parts of the state and connecting with the major rail lines of Canada.

The two steamers of the overnight line from Boston to Portland, *Governor Dingley* and *Bay State*, were not only different from the steamers of the other lines in that they were larger, they were also very different from each other. During the 1890s the Portland Line had produced two fine sisterships, *Portland* (1890) and *Bay State* (1895). Like the steamers of the other lines, *Portland* and *Bay State* were wooden-hulled sidewheelers. But at nearly 300 feet in length they were considerably larger than any of the other Maine Coast steamers. With this greater length they were able to carry a row of staterooms aft of the Pilot House for about half the length of their Gallery Decks (the second passenger deck). Although the greater efficiency of feathering sidewheels had by then been clearly demonstrated, both *Portland* and *Bay State* carried the usual large radial sidewheels with big decorated paddle-boxes.

With these two large sidewheelers in commission by 1895, the Portland Line was operating two well-matched steamers. But only three years later *Portland* was lost in what has become known as one of the most tragic marine accidents in New England waters. On the evening of Saturday, November 26, 1898, in an era before reliable weather reports were available, *Portland* made her regular evening departure from Boston and headed northward up the coast. The weather indeed looked threatening enough for her sister vessel, *Bay State*, to remain at her dock in Portland. Severe weather was not unusual along this coast, however, and Capt. Blanchard of *Portland*, unaware that New England was to experience one of the fiercest storms recorded up to that time, saw no reason to cancel his scheduled sailing. On her way up the coast, *Portland* was sighted by other vessels as far north as Cape Ann about midnight, but after that she was never seen again. What happened to *Portland* during that night can never be known, because no one on board survived.

In its determination to produce a steamer less vulnerable to the Maine coast's unpredictatable storms, the Portland Line replaced their lost steamer with the steel-hulled propeller-driven *Governor Dingley*, which turned out to be a cross between a coastal steamboat and a small ocean liner. Nearly 325 feet in overall length, carrying nearly 200 staterooms, and measuring 3826 gross tons, *Governor Dingley* was far larger than any other steamer on the Maine coast. Not only was her hull of steel (some-

thing considered almost a sacrilege in Maine, where lumber was still a major local product), but the steel structure was carried up to her Main Deck as well. Aft on the Main Deck, instead of the open and often vulnerable Quarter Deck customary on coastal overnight steamers, *Governor Dingley* sported the counter stern more typical of the design of small ocean steamers of the era.

Above the Main Deck, however, *Governor Dingley* was still a steamboat, though like the smaller Bangor boats, she carried two full passenger decks, a Saloon Deck and a Gallery Deck, with her Pilot House placed on the deck above that. *Governor Dingley* was also the first Maine steamer to locate her dining area on the Quarter Deck rather than in the hold or forward between the rows of staterooms on the Saloon Deck, as was the case on all of the other local steamers. As she was built, there were staterooms along the bulkheads on either side of the dining area. Later, however, these staterooms were removed, so that passengers could view the passing scenery, or perhaps less happily the rising and falling horizon, while dining.

In spite of her strong steel construction and

Sagadahoc pulling away from a landing along the Kennebec. (From the Collection of Frank E. Claes)

Ransom B. Fuller, which replaced *Sagadahoc* on the Kennebec route.

Ransom B. Fuller making her way up the Kennebec. (From the Collection of Frank E. Claes)

The small sternwheel steamer *Della Collins*, which met the night boats at Gardiner and took transfer passengers and cargo to landings farther up the Kennebec River as far as Augusta.

ocean-type hull, *Governor Dingley* was perceived to carry too much superstructure for proper stability, for she developed a tendency to roll in almost any sea.

With the new steel-hulled propeller steamer *Governor Dingley*, the largest and most modern of the Maine Coast steamers, operating opposite the wooden-hulled sidewheeler *Bay State* (which was only four years older), the Portland Line obviously no longer boasted a well-matched pair.

The four overnight steamboat lines acquired by Charles W. Morse and combined as the Eastern Steamship Company formed an integral part of the lives of the people along the Maine Coast. In the era before the automobile, any local merchant going up to Boston to order new supplies or any adult son with a job in Boston heading home for the holidays or for occasional weekends, usually travelled aboard the night boat to Boston. Similarly, families from Boston, or even from as far away as New York or Philadelphia headed "Down East" to a summer home on the Maine Coast generally travelled by overnight steamer.

A trip to Boston on one of the night boats of Morse's Eastern Steamship Company was always an exciting event. If families were not taking the trip together, often the whole family would accompany the traveller to the landing. The younger members often enjoyed maintaining a watch up the river in order to be the first to see the steamer rounding the bend. As the steamer came closer one could hear the familiar regular beat of the sidewheels, which became steadily slower until she approached the landing. Then there would be a great swell of white water as she reversed her wheels and glided to a stop, always absolutely accurately, right alongside the wharf.

Boarding the steamer one ascended the narrow gangplank into the Quarter Deck Entrance Hall aft on the Main Deck. This area was usually of stained wood, with a floor covered in bright colored rubber tiles. Here, behind a caged window, was the Purser's Office where the passengers obtained the key to their stateroom (which usually cost a dollar more than the dollar-fifty fare for the passage). Up the wide staircase from the Quarter Deck the passenger arrived in the elegant lounge at the after end of the Saloon Deck between the rows of staterooms on either side of the steamer. Aboard the newer steamers, this area was two decks in height, with a second deck of staterooms, called the Gallery Deck, surrounded by a railing, over

Bay State, which ran opposite the larger steel-hulled *Governor Dingley* between Boston and Portland. (Steamship Historical Society Collection, University of Baltimore)

the Saloon Deck. Although the Maine Coast steamers were neither so large nor so lavishly decorated as some of the steamers on Long Island Sound, their lounge areas were nevertheless elegantly furnished, with rows of plush-covered chairs and deep Turkish carpetting. Passengers on a coastal overnight steamer could always feel that they were travelling in style.

Compared with the Saloon Deck lounge, passengers might find their private staterooms somewhat Spartan. Most contained only narrow double-decker berths, a stool, and a stand with a water pitcher and a glass, with little space for anything else.

Once passengers had deposited their bags in the staterooms, they might wish to walk out on deck. Unless a passenger had boarded at one of the major landings, such as Bath or Rockland, the steamer would not have remained long at the landing and would quickly be underway again. Once on deck, the fresh breeze, the beautiful scenery along the Penobscot or the Kennebec, the syncopated sounds of a sidewheel steamer coursing her way through the water, all gave the passenger an exciting sense of having emerged in a fascinating world very different from that of usual daily life.

The sound of a gong in the distance informed passengers that dinner was being served. On most of the Maine coast steamers passengers found seats at at one of the two or three long tables set up in the forward part of the Saloon Deck. One former passenger recorded his memories of a night on the steamer *Kennebec* as follows:

> There was a single long table with fifty people, more or less, lined on both sides of it. An amazing variety of eatables awaited them. Everything was on the board at once.... There were platters of steak, of ham and eggs, of sausage and liver, and fried ham. There were flapjacks and maple syrup, "home-fried" potatoes, cold meats, and garden truck. For dessert there were strawberries or raspberries or blueberries, as the season might be. Plenty of Cream to go with them. Likewise a variety of cakes, cookies, doughnuts, tarts.[1]

By the time dinner was over the steamer would have completed her river landings and steamed out

16

Governor Dingley (Steamship Historical Society Collection, University of Baltimore)

Calvin Austin of the International Line. (From the Collection of Frank E. Claes)

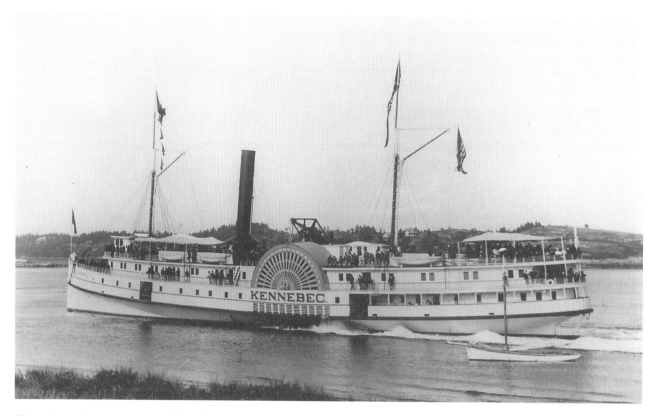

Kennebec, shown here making her way up the Kennebec River, was sold to the Enterprise Line on Long Island Sound in 1905. (From the Collection of Frank E. Claes)

into the Atlantic. On this part of the trip on most nights a passenger, standing on the deck in the dark under the stars, lulled by the regular splashing of the sidewheels and soothed by the peaceful sounds of the sea, could enjoy a serenely beautiful experience before heading into the stateroom for a sound restful sleep as the steamer rolled gently in the ocean swells. There were other times to be sure, although thankfully not very many, when once the steamer had ventured out into the cold Atlantic, passengers might spend a terrifying night with their fingers dug into any handy railing in fear for their lives and praying that the wildly bouncing and pitching steamer would survive long enough to get them to Boston in the morning. With exceptions few enough to count, these staunchly built steamers did, of course, steam snappily into Boston the following morning, usually paddling up to the wharf right on schedule as though there had been nothing unusual about the voyage from Maine. And chances are there had in fact been nothing really unusual about the trip.

As Morse had predicted, the Eastern Steamship Company, his newly formed combine, proved prosperous. Whether or not he actually understood

it, Morse had chosen the ideal time to invest in the steamship business. The turn of the century came between the time when a fast-growing industrial and urban American East Coast was producing a class of people who could afford to travel or to spend their summers either at the shore or in the mountains, most particularly somewhere in northern New England, and the time starting about two decades later when these people would more likely be driving to their destinations in an automobile. The turn of the century also came between the time when the burgeoning business firms and factories of New England were finding that the most efficient form of transportation for products shipped to areas along the irregular coast of Maine inaccessible by rail was by steamboat and the time when gasoline-powered trucks could deliver these products directly to their destinations. In short, during the first two decades of the twentieth century, more than at any other time, Americans and their industrial products were travelling on overnight steamboats, and Charles W. Morse arrived on the scene just at the right time to catch steamboat travel at its crest.

Justifiably optimistic about his company's potential, Morse requested, and was granted, author-

18

ity for the Eastern Steamship Company to issue $3,000,000 in stocks and another $3,000,000 in bonds. From this $6,000,000 of new capital (of which half was essentially borrowed money), $1,730,000 was used to repay Morse for his original outlay. The rest was intended for building new steamers, for Morse's ultimate objective was to provide each of his Maine Coast lines with large steel-hulled steamers similar to the new *Governor Dingley* of the Portland Line.

The first new steamer added to Morse's fleet, however, was another wooden-hulled sidewheeler with a walking-beam engine, for *Ransom B. Fuller*, the steamer built for the Kennebec Line in 1902, was already under construction when Morse purchased the company. *Ransom B. Fuller*, perhaps not surprisingly, was the last wooden-hulled sidewheel night boat produced for a Maine coast service and probably the last for any line on the Atlantic coast. Considering that the Portland Line, with the shortest run, had produced the modern steel-hulled propeller steamer *Governor Dingley* in 1899, both the Bangor Line's *City of Rockland* of 1901 and the Kennebec Line's *Ransom B. Fuller* of 1902, with their wooden hulls and walking-beam engines, have to be seen as out-of-date even when they were built.

Once the new *Ransom B. Fuller* started running on the Kennebec Line opposite *Kennebec*, the older *Sagadahoc* was no longer needed. With other unused steamers, especially *Penobscot*, now available from the various lines in Morse's combine, there was no advantage to maintaining *Sagadahoc* even as a spare. Since *Sagadahoc* by 1902 had been in service for thirty-six years, one might have expected her to be retired or sent to the bone yard. But the staunch old

steamer still had another long career ahead of her. The following year Morse sold her to the Montauk Line where, renamed *Greenport*, she alternated with that line's *Shinnecock* on an overnight route between New York and Eastern Long Island. Apparently the Montauk Line was unable to maintain its payments, however, for in 1908 *Greenport* was returned to Morse, who placed her on one of his Hudson River routes. She was not retired until 1916, by which time she had been running for fifty years.

Soon after setting up the Eastern Steamship Company, Morse was ready to begin his program of replacing the older wooden-hulled sidewheel steamers on his Maine coast lines with more modern steel-hulled vessels. The first, ordered for the International Division, was named *Calvin Austin* for the President of Eastern Steamship. The new *Calvin Austin* was in many ways a conscious copy of the Portland Line's *Governor Dingley*, although she kept the more typical open Quarter Deck aft on her Maine Deck. Her dimensions and her triple expansion reciprocating engine were virtually identical to those of *Governor Dingley*, and, like her, she had a steel hull and steel construction up to the Main Deck and two full decks of staterooms. With her total of 224 staterooms, more than twice the number on any of the older steamers on the International Line, *Calvin Austin* probably had the largest passenger capacity in proportion to her size of any American overnight boat other than those of the Fall River Line or the Albany night line.

With her more graceful sheer and her somewhat better proportioned single black smokestack, *Calvin Austin*, though similar to *Governor Dingley* in most respects, was by far the handsomer steamer. In

J. T. Morse replaced *Mount Desert* on the day route between Rockland and Bar Harbor in 1904.

19

City of Rockland

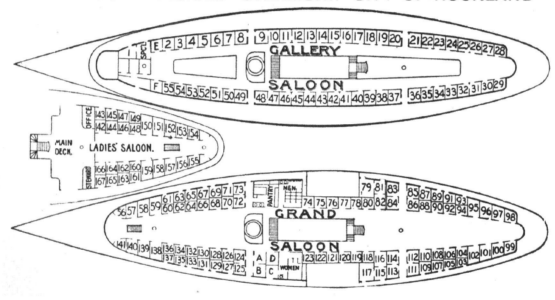

STATEROOM DIAGRAM—STEAMSHIP CITY OF ROCKLAND

This stateroom diagram of *City of Rockland* shows a fairly typical plan of a Maine Coast overnight steamer.

a.) The shorter plan in the center shows the after part of the first deck above the hull, called the "Main Deck." Forward on this deck (and therefore not shown) are a large cargo area, part of the crew's quarters, and part of the engine housing. In the after section shown here, called the Quarter Deck, is an Entrance Hall (where the words "Main Deck" appear), which is where passengers board the steamer. Here are the Purser's Office and a stairway leading to the Grand Saloon above. Aft of the Entrance Hall is a cabin area, traditionally labeled "Ladies' Saloon," though the cabins were not necessarily reserved for women travellers. On some of Eastern Steamship's larger vessels, a formal Dining Room was located in this area.

b.) The deck above that, the "Grand Saloon" or sometimes called the "Saloon Deck," has a double row of staterooms on either side and a public area down the center, divided into two parts by the engine housing amidships, and with open balustraded wells to the deck above both fore and aft. On *City of Rockland*, as on many of the earlier Maine Coast steamers, the dining area consisted of tables set up in the forward part of the public area on this deck.

c.) On the Gallery Saloon (or "Gallery Deck") above are the Pilot House forward, a few rooms for officers, and only single rows of staterooms on each side (allowing greater outboard deck space for lifeboats) with the balustraded wells opening to the Saloon Deck below between the two rows of staterooms. Over the public area of the Gallery Deck was a slightly arched dome with a continuous row of small windows to let light into the central parts of the steamer.

C. W. Morse of the Hudson River Night Line was one of the largest inland water steamers in the world. (Steamship Historical Society Collection, University of Baltimore Library)

fact, she was one of the most attractive steamers ever to operate on the Maine coast.

In case the question should be asked why the first new steel steamer of the Eastern Steamship Company was named for the company's President and not for Morse himself, it should be noted that a far larger steamer, one of the largest inland water steamers in America in fact, to be named *C. W. Morse*, was then under construction for Morse's Albany night line.

Although *Calvin Austin* had been ordered especially to replace *St. Croix*, the steamer on the International Division that had never proved very satisfactory, unexpected events were to make it more expedient to adopt a different plan. During the morning of July 8, 1902, as *Cumberland* headed out of Boston harbor through a pea soup fog, she was struck just forward of her pilot house by the incoming fruit liner, *Admiral Farragut*. In a daring if somewhat dangerous decision, *Cumberland*'s captain, to avoid allowing his steamer to be lost by sinking where she was in deep water, refused all assistance at the scene and instead put his stricken steamer about to head her back to the pier in Boston through the fog. Fortunately he was successful and was able to disembark

all of his passengers before *Cumberland* finally went down in shallow water.

Though *Cumberland* had not been seriously damaged, since *Calvin Austin* would be ready to join the line the following season, the company elected to abandon *Cumberland* to the underwriters and to keep *St. Croix* on the line a few more years. Meanwhile *Penobscot*, the idle spare steamer of the Bangor Line, was placed on the International route on *Cumberland*'s schedule. Later that summer the insurance company sold *Cumberland*, as is, to the Joy Line on Long Island Sound, where, repaired and renamed *Larchmont*, she was to figure in a far more serious accident five years later.

In 1903, when the sparkling new 322-foot steel-hulled propeller steamer *Calvin Austin* became the running mate of the twenty-one-year-old wooden-hulled sidewheeler, *State of Maine*, and the cranky wooden-hulled propeller steamer, *St. Croix*, Morse's International Division found itself operating with a rather odd mix of steamers.

Over the next several years there was to be considerable rivalry between the similar steamers *Calvin Austin* of the International Division and *Gov-*

Edgemont, shown here on Narragansett Bay, had been *State of Maine* on the International Line before she was sold to the Joy Line in 1904.

ernor *Dingley* of the Portland Division. Once each year these two fine steamers had the chance to face off with one another. Every Labor Day *Governor Dingley* was sent on an extra daylight trip from Boston to Portland in order to make the heavily booked sailings from Portland on both Sunday and Monday evenings of the holiday weekend, and this extra trip happened to coincide with the regular daylight Boston-to-Portland leg of *Calvin Austin*'s run to St. John. Although any official race would have been strictly against the rules, an unofficial record shows that *Calvin Austin*'s best time from Boston to Portland was six hours flat, whereas *Governor Dingley*, running light, as she would on Labor Day, once completed the course in five hours and fifty minutes.

Morse's next addition to his Eastern Steamship fleet was a new steamer for the day route from

Rockland across Penobscot Bay to Bar Harbor. On June 10, 1904, the smart new *J. T. Morse*, named for the President's uncle, James T. Morse, who was also Treasurer of the company, made her first sailing, replacing the older *Mt. Desert*. Although as a wooden-hulled sidewheeler with a walking-beam engine, *J. T.Morse* might be considered somewhat old-fashioned in 1904, with her enclosed feathering sidewheels and clean well-proportioned lines, she was nevertheless a beautiful small steamboat. *J. T. Morse* was to make the early morning sailings from Rockland every day during the season for nearly thirty years, in the process becoming one of the best-loved steamers on the Maine coast.

Although *J. T. Morse* was immediately popular, *Mt. Desert*'s deeply devoted following among Penobscot Bay regulars was saddened by her departure. Although the reliable old *Mt. Desert* had been covering her route for twenty-five years when *J. T. Morse* came to take her place, she was still to see a few more years of service. Sold first for an excursion run out of Boston, she was purchased a few years later by the Starin Line in New York. Renamed *Arion*, she served on several of Starin's excursion routes but mainly between Manhattan and Starin's park on Glen Island, near New Rochelle, New York, on Long Island Sound. She was finally laid up permanently at the end of the season of 1913. On May 28, 1904, the same day that *J. T. Morse* was taken out for her trial runs in Boston Harbor and Massachusetts Bay, the big new steel-hulled sidewheel night boat, *C. W. Morse*, made her first sailing from New York to Albany. At the time *C. W. Morse* was the second-largest inland water steamer in America (after the slightly larger *Priscilla* of the Fall River Line).

It was also in 1904 that *State of Maine* was sold to the Joy Line, where, renamed *Edgemont*, she was to serve on the line's New York-to-Providence route opposite *Larchmont* (a. *Cumberland*), her former running mate on the International Line. The Joy Line had lost a steamer to fire early that year and needed a replacement as soon as possible. The company's managers had been so pleased with *Cumberland*'s performace that they went to C. W. Morse and specifically asked to buy her sistership, *State of Maine*. Although *State of Maine* was in service at the time and not for sale, Morse obliged. It is not clear why Morse was willing to sell this steamer. She was needed on the International route, and Morse certainly did not need the money. The fact that the Joy Line found it necessary to send the steamer for a major two-month engine overhaul at the height of the season, shortly after they acquired her, might help explain Morse's acquiescence, however. *Penobscot*, which was of about the same size and vintage, if not nearly so stable a sea boat, was again transferred to the International Line to take over *State of Maine*'s scheduled sailings that season. But this arrangement left Eastern Steamship without a spare boat during the season of 1904.

State of Maine had not been running long on her new route between New York and Providence before Morse had serious cause to regret his having parted with her so easily. On July 26, 1904, *City of Rockland*, approaching Penobscot Bay in an early morning fog, struck hard on a rocky ledge near the

Larchmont, shown here on Narragansett Bay, had been *Cumberland* of the International Line before she was sold to the Joy Line in 1902.
(Steamship Historical Society Collection, University of Baltimore Library)

entrance to the bay. Although her captain, Marcus Pierce, was able to back her off successfully, as her hull had been punctured, *City of Rockland* sank before he could get her safely into Rockland. Fortunately the water was not deep where she went down and much of her superstructure remained above water, so transferring her passengers to the small boats that came out during the morning to help was not difficult.

Although at the time Eastern Steamship had reason to fear that their virtually new *City of Rockland* had been lost, the salvage company was able to raise her, albeit with considerable difficulty. With a temporary patch in her hull, *City of Rockland* was towed to the Atlantic Works in Boston, where a close examination revealed that, although she could be repaired and returned to service, she would require major reconstruction. Not only was there a thirty-foot gash in her hull, but after several days partly under water much of her interior had also been badly damaged. Carpets, bedding, and much of her electrical system had to be replaced, as well as a fair amount of her interior wood planking.

With *City of Rockland* off the route for the rest of the 1904 season, Morse had to borrow the similar *Ransom B. Fuller* from his Kennebec line to run on the Penobscot route opposite *City of Bangor*. To re-place *Ransom B. Fuller* on the Kennebec line, *Penobscot* was borrowed from the International route. With *State of Maine* already sold, the International Division had to function that season with only *Calvin Austin* and *St. Croix* maintaining a curtailed schedule of sailings.

In 1905 Morse capped his Maine marine collection by acquiring the Rockland, Blue Hill, and Ellsworth Steamboat Company, another line of small steamers that met the Bangor boats at Rockland in the early morning and carried passengers and cargo to various landings on the other side of Penobscot Bay. The combined operations of this line and the route of *J. T. Morse* became known as the Mt. Desert and Blue Hill Division of the Eastern Steamship Company.

By 1905 the various routes of the Eastern Steamship Company were functioning smoothly. The fact that in the following year the company was able to return 8.9% dividends to its stockholders seemed to substantiate Morse's original contention that these lines would operate both more efficiently and more profitably when they were united under a single management.

1. Marc T. Greene, "The Old Home Ship," *Ships and the Sea*, Fall, 1957, p. 39.

II. The Metropolitan Line: 1905-1907

One day in July, 1905, C. W. Morse appeared in the Boston office of H. M. Whitney, the President of the Metropolitan Line and offered him $3,000,000 for his company. Whitney, who knew that the marine and wharf assets of the Metropolitan Line had been evaluated as recently as May, 1904, at $1,222,836, apparently needed only a few minutes to consider Morse's offer before agreeing to sell.

The Metropolitan Steamship Company operated cargo steamers between Boston and New York. With three modern freight steamers in operation and another in reserve with steam up, this line scheduled three sailings a week from both Boston and New York and occasional extra sailings when necessary. Founded in 1860 and managed privately by members of the Whitney family, who had been the sole owners of the company since 1872, this line, which had been rewarding its investors with regular 10% annual dividends for many years, was considered one of the most profitable steamship operations in the northeast.

Metropolitan Line steamers were known for making their scheduled sailings in virtually any weather. The usual route of these vessels took them from New York through Long Island Sound and Vineyard Sound and then out around Cape Cod to Boston. But on many nights when fog, ice, or heavy weather kept other Long Island Sound steamers tied to their piers, the Metropolitan Line freighters often headed south from Manhattan through the Narrows into the Atlantic and around Long Island to Boston.

The Metropolitan Line enjoyed a virtual monopoly on the New York-to-Boston run. A few competitors had appeared over the years, but none had lasted long. At the time Morse purchased the company, the Joy Line was operating two steamers between New York and Boston carrying passengers as well as cargo. But their steamers both dated from the 1870s and required a full twenty-four hours for the trip. The Metropolitan Line had no need to take the threat posed by the Joy Line very seriously.

Since all four of Morse's Eastern Steamship overnight lines brought products not only from various parts of Maine but also from much of eastern Canada into the port of Boston, one can understand that the highly profitable Metropolitan Line, which could provide Morse with a steamer connection between Boston and New York, would be a valuable addition to his operations.

Once Morse had acquired the line, the Metropolitan Steamship Company registered in Massachusetts was dissolved, and a new Metropolitan Steamship Company registered in Maine was established. Although Morse now became its Chairman and Calvin Austin its President, the Metropolitan Line remained a separate corporation and was not at that time brought under the aegis of Morse's Eastern Steamship Company.

With his purchase of the Metropolitan Line, Morse acquired not only the coveted steamer connection between Boston and the markets of New York but also the line's four staunchly built cargo steamers. The iron-hulled *H. F. Dimock* (1884), *Herman Winter* (1887), named for the prominent naval architect who designed all of these steamers, and *H. M. Whitney* (1890), all 271.8 in length, were virtually sisterships. The similar *James S. Whitney* (1900), a steel-hulled vessel, was slightly larger. Also in the Metropolitan Line's fleet were the wooden-hulled freighters, *Glaucus* and *Neptune*, two of the three steamers with which the company had started its service in 1866. *Glaucus* and *Neptune*, however, had been in lay-up in the Erie Basin, Brooklyn, for so many years that one marine reporter suspected they had grown roots. As they were no longer fit for service, Morse was to sell both for scrap soon after he purchased the company.

It would appear that Charles W. Morse now had everything he needed for a prosperous business. He controlled virtually all coastal shipping between the State of Maine and the port of Boston, and now he also owned a line of cargo steamers known to be consistently profitable connecting Boston with New York.

The marine world was stunned, therefore, when in August, 1905, only a few weeks after he had purchased the Metropolitan Line, Morse announced that he had ordered the construction of two large and very fast passenger steamers to operate directly be-

Herman Winter, one of the four cargo steamers of the Metropolitan Line between New York and Boston. *H. F. Dimock* and *H. M. Whitney* were similar.
(Steamship Historical Society Collection, Universty of Baltimore Library)

tween New York and Boston. Before the completion of the Cape Cod Canal in 1914 it had not been considered feasible to operate passenger vessels between New York and Boston, since the necessity of sailing all the way around Cape Cod added too many hours—and not very comfortable hours—to the trip. For nearly a century passengers travelling by water between New York and Boston had boarded one of the Long Island Sound steamers which sailed from Manhattan in the early evening and tied up at some port on Narragansett Bay about 5:30 the following morning. From this port—usually Providence or Fall River—which was not far from Boston, passengers transferred to a train which brought them into Boston about 8:00 A.M.

Morse, however, announced that he would produce ships fast enough to steam from New York directly to Boston on roughly the same schedule as the steamer-and-rail routes provided by the Long Island Sound lines. To achieve this exceptional speed, his new steamers were to be powered by the recently-developed Parsons turbine engines. Although several turbine-powered vessels had been proved both fast and efficient in Great Britain, turbine engines had yet to be tried in America. At that time the Cunard Line,

which already had one successful turbine-driven ship in operation, was constructing the two large turbine-powered ocean liners, *Mauretania* and *Lusitania*, which the company confidently predicted (correctly, as it happened) would become the fastest ships on the Atlantic. Morse, therefore, turned to naval architects in Scotland (William Denny and Brothers, Ltd., of Dumbarton) to design the hulls for his proposed new Boston steamers, although the firm of W. and A. Fletcher, which was to build the turbine engines for Morse's new steamers, was also involved in the hull design.

Since one of his sons at the time was enrolled at Harvard and the other at Yale, Morse chose to name his two new steamers *Harvard* and *Yale*. When Morse signed the contracts with John Roach's shipyard in Chester, Pennsylvania, to construct the hulls for his new steamers, with W. and A. Fletcher of Hoboken to equip each of them with three powerful turbine engines together producing 10,000 Horsepower, and with John Englis and Son of Greenpoint, Brooklyn, to complete their superstructures and joiner work, his instructions were to build vessels that "would be beyond any class of ships heretofore constructed," and

James M. Whitney, last of the four cargo steamers of the Metropolitan Line, was somewhat larger than the earlier three steamers of that line.
(Steamship Historical Society Collection, University of Baltimore Library)

capable of maintaining a minimum speed of twenty-one knots (or about twenty-four miles per hour, considerably faster than any American-flag steamship at that time). Apparently expense was not an issue, for these contracts stipulated that Morse's new steamers would each cost $1,225,000 to produce.[1]

As there were no turbine-powered vessels in America, Calvin Austin, the President of Eastern Steamship, and Andrew Fletcher, the President of W. and A. Fletcher, travelled to Great Britain in 1905 to study turbine engines first-hand, both in factories and in operating steamships. Andrew Fletcher, in fact, spent several months at the plant of the Parsons company in Wallsend-on-Tyne, learning every detail of the construction of turbine engines. He later made trips on the few turbine-driven steamers which had been in service for a year or more to try to determine what kinds of problems might have developed in operation.

Before investing such a large sum in their projected new liners for the Metropolitan Line, C. W. Morse and Calvin Austin decided to experiment with a smaller turbine-powered steamer for Eastern's International Division. This steamer, which was to resemble *Calvin Austin* and *Governor Dingley*, was to

be named *Governor Cobb*, for William Cobb, who was then Governor of the State of Maine and also a member of the Board of the Eastern Steamship Company. Morse turned to Roach's yard for her steel hull, to W. and A. Fletcher for her turbine engine, and to John Englis and Son for her joiner work, the companies with which he had contracted for the hull, engines, and superstructures of the much larger *Harvard* and *Yale*.

Morse's announcement that he was about to establish a new passenger line between New York and Boston with steamers so fast they would be able to pull out of their pier in Manhattan at 5:00 P.M., steam overnight the length of Long Island Sound and around Cape Cod to deliver passengers in downtown Boston by 8:00 the following morning, was certainly a bold and brilliant business venture, but it was also, under the circumstances, somewhat foolhardy. The primary water-and-rail route between New York and Boston at that time was via the prestigious Fall River Line, whose elegantly appointed steamers *Priscilla* and *Puritan* were two of the three largest inland-water vessels in America. (The other was *C. W. Morse* of the Albany night line.) The Fall River Line was part of the

27

City of Augusta, the sternwheeler built in 1906 to replace *Della Collins* on the Upper Kennebec River, was a disappointment until she was rebuilt.
(Marine Museum at Fall River, Massachusetts)

Monhegan, which ran opposite *Mineola* on the route between Portland and Rockland.

New England Navigation Company (later known as the New England Steamship Company), which also operated several other water-and-rail routes between New York and Boston, especially the Providence Line, whose summer steamers, *Plymouth* and *Pilgrim*, were the winter boats of the great Fall River Line. The New England Navigation Company was in turn a subsidiary of the New York, New Haven, and Hartford Railroad (better known as the New Haven Railroad), on whose Board sat the formidable financier J. Pierpont Morgan.

It was well-known that J. Pierpont Morgan and Charles Mellen, Morgan's hand-picked President of the New Haven Railroad, were then in the process of creating a monopoly of transportation systems (railroads, steamships, and trolleys) operating between New York and Boston. In announcing his plans to inaugurate a new steamship line—with steamers fast enough to bring passengers directly into the port of Boston at the same hour that passengers who had taken the Fall River Line steamer and transferred to a train at five-thirty in the morning were arriving there by rail—Charles W. Morse had not merely tweaked the lion's tail, he had stalked right into its cage!

Morgan could countenance no opposition to his own plans for a monopoly of the New York-to-Boston traffic and lost no time in launching an all-out counter-offensive against Morse. On September 15, 1905, just three weeks after Morse's announcement, Morgan and Mellen summoned an emergency evening meeting of the Board of Directors of the New Haven Railroad. At this meeting Mellen, obviously speaking for Morgan, recommended that the New England Navigation Company build not merely two but three new steamers as large and as fast as *Yale* and *Harvard* to operate between New York and Boston in competition with Morse's Metropolitan Line. With the resources of the New Haven Railroad behind it, this line could afford to operate at a loss, with rates considerably lower than Morse's, until it had forced the Metropolitan Line out of business. The New Haven's directors had no intention of starting a permanent steamer line between New York and Boston. Rather shortsightedly, it would seem in retrospect (since plans for building the Cape Cod Canal had already been announced), they expected to run their New York-Boston line only long enough to clear the field of any competition to their own Fall River Line.

At Mellen's suggestion these three steamers were to be constructed as freighters with the hope that the New Haven could bring down Morse simply by siphoning off Metropolitan's cargo contracts. They would, however, be designed to allow easy conversion to passenger service should the directors decide that passenger steamers were called for. As plans for these three super-freighters were being drawn up, the question naturally arose whether they should be equipped, like *Yale* and *Harvard*, with turbine engines. The conservative engineers of the New England Navigation Company, J. Howland Gardiner and Stevenson Taylor, demurred at investing such a large amount of capital in a system as yet untried. In the end the New Haven compromised by placing triple-screw turbine engines in just one of their three steamers. The other two were equipped with very powerful versions of the more typical twin-screw triple-expansion reciprocating engines.

All three of these new fast freighters were constructed at the Cramp shipyard in Philadelphia. Their engines were designed and built by the Quintard Iron Works of New York, which should not be surprising, since Stevenson Taylor, who had designed the highly successful engines for all of the large Fall River Line sidewheelers, had recently left W. and A. Fletcher to become Senior Vice President of Quintard. As had been planned, two of these steamers, to be named *Bunker Hill* and *Massachusetts*, were equipped with twin-screw reciprocating engines developing 7000 Horsepower, considerably less power than *Yale* or *Harvard*. The third steamer, to be named *Old Colony*, was equipped with triple-screw direct-acting turbines producing only 5000 Horsepower.

With the announcement of this second new express steamer line between New York and Boston, J. Pierpont Morgan and the New Haven Railroad had thrown down the gauntlet for a fight to the finish with Morse's Metropolitan Line.

Morse should have understood that, in spite of his recently-acquired wealth and the success of his growing marine empire, he was not in a position to take on either the New Haven Railroad or J. Pierpont Morgan. Instead of backing off to a position from which he would not be so blatantly inviting Morgan's powerful opposition, Morse elected to challenge Morgan openly by creating his own maritime monopoly, not merely in New England, but of all shipping along the Atlantic Coast.

Morse began in February, 1906, by purchasing the Clyde Line, a major steamship company operating twenty-three ships on a variety of routes along

Governor Cobb, built in 1906 to replace *St. Croix* on the International Line, was the first turbine-powered vessel in the United States. (Marine Museum at Fall River, Massachusetts)

the Atlantic Coast, mostly between Boston or New York and Charleston or Jacksonville. (That season Morse was therefore able to borrow *Huron*, one of the Clyde Line's smaller steamers, to take over *Penobscot*'s schedule on the International Division.) A few weeks later Morse bought the New York and Texas Steamship Company (better known as the Mallory Line, and renamed Mallory Steamship Company by Morse), which operated eleven ships on a route from New York to Galveston with a stop along the way at Key West for connections to Havana. For this company, known as the major carrier of raw cotton to the factories in the north, the former owners, still mostly members of the Mallory family, were pleased to accept the $9,000,000 offered by Morse.

Morse wisely maintained the original personnel of both of these companies, wherever possible, both in management and on the ships. In both companies the new boards consisted of several former board members or former executives, with the addition of a few of Morse's people, and with Calvin Austin as President and C. W. Morse as Chairman (as was the case in both the Eastern and the Metropolitan steamship companies).

In 1906 Morse also found one more Maine coast steamship line that he seemed to have overlooked in his sweep of the field in 1901. About 1897 Captain I. E. (for Isaac Edson) Archibald had started operating the small (95.8') *Merryconeag* for passengers and cargo on the open-ocean route between Portland and Rockland with stops at various landings along the way. As business improved, Capt. Archibald added the larger *Mineola* (121') in 1901 to offer daily sailings in each direction, at least during the busier season. Two years later, he sold *Merryconeag* and replaced her with the new *Monhegan* (128'), a substantial small steamer particularly well adapted to the occasional heavy weather she often encountered along this stretch of rugged coast.[2]

The $75,000 Morse offered for the line was

30

apparently sufficient for Captain Archibald to overcome any hesitation he might have harbored about selling this service which he had clearly enjoyed operating. In any event, during the season of 1906 *Monhegan* and *Mineola* began sporting "Eastern Steamship Company" on their bows.

During 1906 Morse had also been active in his program of replacing the older wooden-hulled sidewheelers on his Maine Coast lines with more modern vessels. During that year, while *Governor Cobb* was under construction at Roach's for the International Line (to replace *St. Croix* at last!), Morse turned to the Bath Iron Works in his home town to order the construction of a sleek new 332-foot steel-hulled steamer, to be named *Camden* (one of the landings on Penobscot Bay), for the Bangor Line. This steamer was to have steel construction up to her Main Deck like *Governor Dingley* and *Calvin Austin*, and, like *Governor Cobb*, to be powered by triple-screw direct-acting Parsons turbine engines.

On April 21, 1906, C. W. Morse, Calvin Austin, Governor William Cobb, and Andrew Fletcher, with their wives and families and several invited guests, took the Pennsylvania Railroad's ferry to New Jersey where they boarded a special railroad car to carry them to Chester, Pennsylvania, to attend the launching of *Governor Cobb*. After she was launched, *Governor Cobb* was towed up to the yard of W. and A. Fletcher's in Hoboken where Fletcher installed her turbine engines and John Englis and Son completed her joiner work.

As *Governor Cobb* was the first American-built vessel to be powered with turbine engines, the installation—which involved setting several thousand blades in each of three engines with the precision of the works in a Swiss watch—attracted a great deal of attention from naval architects and marine engineers around the country. No one was more concerned, however, than C. W. Morse, as the success or failure of *Governor Cobb*'s engines could predict success or failure for his *Yale* and *Harvard*.

Governor Cobb was to have three separate turbine engines each turning one of her triple screws. Since the turbines turned their shafts much faster than a reciprocating engine did, it was found that three small propellers were more efficient than one or two larger ones. On *Governor Cobb* (as also later on *Yale*, *Harvard*, *Camden*, and *Belfast*) the central high pres-

Governor Cobb at St. John, New Brunswick. The vessel *Empress* to the left in the photograph ran between St. John and Digby, N. S.
(R. Loren Graham Collection, Steamship Historical Society, University of Baltimore Library)

Camden as she first appeared in 1907 before the steel railing was added at her bow.
(From the Collection of Frank E. Claes)

sure turbine was geared only for a forward movement, whereas the two low pressure turbines on either side were geared for either forward or reverse. It was only later that the officers of these steamers began to realize the disadvantage of this arrangement, for, as it turned out, with no thrust emanating from the center propeller past the rudder, a steamer attempting to slow by reversing her propellers could sometimes become hard to steer.

When *Governor Cobb* emerged from the Fletcher yard on October 17, 1906, for her first trial run up the Hudson River, her engines met every expectation. Developing 5000 Horsepower, she easily worked up to a speed of 21.5 miles per hour (17.5 knots) with no perceptible vibration. This was a rare, even unanticipated, performance for a propeller-driven steamer. Although Andrew Fletcher wanted to conduct further tests, Morse was so pleased with the success of his new steamer that, rather like a child who cannot wait until Christmas, he wanted *Governor Cobb* delivered immediately.

On the first of November, 1906, *Governor*

Cobb pulled out of her berth at the Fletcher yard in Hoboken, steamed up the East River, through Long Island Sound, and around Cape Cod to Boston in just sixteen hours, in the process setting a new record for the New York-Boston run. Before the month was over, *Governor Cobb* had joined *Calvin Austin* on the International Line.

Governor Cobb was more than ten feet shorter than either *Calvin Austin* or *Governor Dingley*, and she carried considerably fewer staterooms than either, 160 as compared with 225 on *Calvin Austin*. It is not clear why this second new steamer for the International Line was designed with a smaller passenger capacity than the earlier one. Perhaps Morse had discovered that the demands of the service did not warrant another steamer with the enormous capacity of *Calvin Austin*. Or perhaps the company hoped that carrying fewer staterooms topsides would lower her center of gravity and allow her more stability, a feature not often counted among the virtues of either *Governor Dingley* or *Calvin Austin*. It appears also that *Governor Cobb* was built with the intention of

32

operating her on the International Line in the summer and chartering her on a regular basis to Henry Flagler in Florida to replace his inadequate *Martinique* on the Key West-Havana route in the winter. (Thus it could be said that *Governor Cobb* was built to replace two different steamers, *St. Croix* in summer, which operated at the extreme northern end of the Atlantic Coast of the United States into another country and *Martinique* in winter, which operated at the extreme southern end of the Atlantic Coast of the United States into another country.)

The overwhelming success of *Governor Cobb's* turbine engines prompted Charles W. Morse to ask the Bath Iron Works to start work on a sistership to *Camden*, which was already under construction at the yard. The second new steamer for the Bangor route was to be named *Belfast* for another of the line's landings on Penobscot Bay. In recognition for the orders for two new turbine-driven sisterships to be built at Bath, for the registration of all of his companies and each of his steamships at Bath, and also for the construction of a large and modern new High School for the city in November, 1906, the Merchants Association of Bath drew up a formal resolution thanking Charles W. Morse for his many generosities to his home city.

Apparently not all of the new steamers Morse produced to serve his home state were received with enthusiastic accolades. For the season of 1906 Morse had the small stern-wheeler *City of Augusta* constructed to replace the aging *Della Collins* on the upper Kennebec. *City of Augusta's* rather unfavorable initial reception on the Kennebec, which resulted in her captain's resignation before she had even completed her first trip, is reported in an article from the *Bath Times*:

The impression seems to be gaining along the waterfront that City of Augusta is somebody's bad mistake.... In respect to speed, the craft is entirely satisfactory, but in other respects, the rivermen say, she is inferior to the old Della Collins, over which the new craft was expected to be a big improvement. The freight deck has insufficient head room for the storage of some of the more bulky freight, such as carriages, which the boat will frequently be called upon to carry. Worst of all the Augusta handles badly. Lacking a keel and having only one

rudder, where sternwheelers customarily have from two to five—the old Della had three and a good keel—the craft does not steer well.... When she is drifting to a dock, with the engine stopped or reversed, the rudder might just as well be suspended from the smoke-stack, for all the effect it has on her wayward course....

When Augusta struck the ledges, her skipper, Capt. Lewis. had already passed in his resignation, to take effect upon her return to her dock in Bath...not wishing to jeopardize in an unmanageable craft the reputation he has earned in a quarter of a century in the pilot house of the Collins....[3]

Needless to say *Della Collins* was back on the route for most of the rest of the 1906 season, while *City of Augusta* returned to McKie's in East Boston for a keel and another rudder and to have her freight deck raised several feet. Before *City of Augusta* came on the route in 1906 the Boston steamers had continued from Bath on to Gardiner, and passengers wishing to proceed farther up the river to other landings as far as Augusta transferred there to *Della Collins*. After *City of Augusta* took over the route, however, the larger steamers began ending their runs at Bath, and *City of Augusta* carried passengers and cargo from there.

On the first of December, 1906, just one month after *Governor Cobb's* delivery, *Yale*, the first of the new Metropolitan Line flyers, was launched at Roach's yard. This time the representatives of the Metropolitan Line, of W. and A. Fletcher, and of John Englis and Son, with their families, friends, and invited guests had not merely a private railroad car for the trip to Chester, they had their own private train. Among the party was President Arthur T. Hadley of Yale University with his wife and their seven-year-old daughter, Laura Beaumont Hadley, who was to christen the new vessel.

The elaborate festivities that accompanied the 1:00 P.M. launch of *Yale* were the production of Orlando Taylor, who had previously served as the General Passenger Agent for the New Haven Railroad's New England Navigation Company, but who had been persuaded to join the Metropolitan Line in a similar capacity just one month earlier (possibly in response to another blandishment of Mr. Morse's cornucopian checkbook). Shortly before the launch, Morse presented young Laura Hadley with a diamond and Yale-

Belfast. By the time *Camden*'s sistership, *Belfast*, came out in 1909, both steamers had steel railings at the bow. (From the Collection of Frank E. Claes)

Camden: Interior view looking aft from the Gallery Deck forward.

Belfast: Interior view of Quarter Deck Entrance Hall from the port side looking forward toward the stairway to the Saloon Deck.
(R. Loren Graham Collection, Steamship Historical Society, University of Baltimore Library)

blue sapphire brooch as a present from the Metropolitan Steamship Company. Then, as *Yale*'s graceful hull slid slowly down the ways, hundreds of spectators, all wearing Yale-blue boutonnieres, vigorously waved the blue Yale banners with which each had been supplied by Mr. Taylor.

The launch of *Massachusetts*, the first of the three fast freighters being built for the competing line of the New England Navigation Company followed at Cramp's yard in Philadelphia eight weeks later on January 29, 1907.

At the launch of *Harvard* at Roach's yard the very next day, the adept hand of impresario Taylor was again evident. Red Carnations served as boutonnieres on this occasion, and the banners waved were of Harvard crimson. The guests were President Charles Eliot of Harvard and his wife, while their daughter, Ruth Eliot, was entrusted with swinging the champagne bottle over the liner's bow. There was no mention, however, of Miss Eliot's having been presented with a ruby-and-diamond brooch.

To centralize the operations of his rapidly expanding shipping empire, in January, 1907, Morse created a new umbrella corporation, the Consolidated Steamship Lines, registered in Maine, of course, to serve as a holding company for his growing collection of steamship lines: the Eastern Steamship Company, the Metropolitan Steamship Company, the Hudson Navigation Company, the Clyde Steamship Company, and the Mallory Steamship Company. In the process Morse removed any doubts that might, however unlikely, have lingered in Morgan's mind that his plan was anything less than a monopoly of steamship operations along the Atlantic Coast.

Once this new corporation had been established, Morse secured authorization to issue $60,000,000 in common stock (some of which was traded to stockholders of the member companies for their original shares) and $60,000,000 in bonds, on which the new company would be obliged to pay regular interest.

With this large amount of other people's money backing him, on February 4, 1907, Morse sought to end the rivalry with Morgan in one grand sweep by making a formal offer to purchase all of the marine properties of the New Haven Railroad—which would have included virtually all of the overnight lines on Long Island Sound, among them the prestigious

Camden's triple-screw turbine engines.

Fall River Line—for $20,000,000. At another hastily summoned special meeting of the New Haven's Board of Directors to deal with this unexpected offer, Charles Mellen, the railroad's President, who evaluated the New Haven's marine properties at about five million dollars (based on a thorough analysis of each of the company's steamers by Stevenson Taylor less than one year earlier), was of the opinion that the Board should accept Morse's enormously inflated offer. The railroad's large collection of steamship lines was, in any event, only minimally profitable. And given the enormous outlays the railroad had been making in recent years in response to Morgan's monopolistic mania, Mellen felt that Morse's $20,000,000 could be helpful in unloading some of the New Haven's burdensome debt.

J. Pierpont Morgan, however, did not agree with Mellen. In his opinion a railroad whose future depended on the creation of a complete transportation monopoly did not sell anything. If other Board members had different views to express, they were swept aside too rapidly to be recorded. Morgan said not to sell, so the railroad did not sell. (As Charles Mellen once explained, when asked the name of the New Haven's current Chairman of the Board, "Wherever Mr. Morgan sat was the Chair.") Morgan did allow one small concession. As a sot to Morse, the New Haven agreed to sell him the New York-to-Boston operation of the Joy Line, which the railroad had purchased secretly two years before. Morse paid the railroad $350,000 for the Boston Joy Line, but why Morse was willing to buy this line at any price is a mystery, since these antique steamers could not possibly have survived once Morse's modern *Yale* and *Harvard* were in operation covering the same route in little more than half the time. In any event, once Morse owned the Boston Joy Line, all he did with it was to put the line out of its misery a few months earlier.

Morgan's advice to the Board of the New Haven Railroad was not only to refuse to sell but also to buy! The best way to prevent Morse from creating a shipping monopoly, Morgan reasoned, was to buy up any available coastal steamship lines before Morse could buy them. The next few months witnessed a frenetic buying spree during which both Morse and the New Haven Railroad offered outrageously high prices for any marine properties in order to acquire them as quickly as possible before the other could buy them.

On February 14, just five days after learning of the New Haven's refusal to sell him its marine subsidiaries, Morse purchased the New York and Cuba Mail Line (better known as the Ward Line) and added this company to his Consolidated Steamship Company. One week later on February 21 the New Haven puchased the Boston and Philadelphia Steamship Company (also known as the Winsor Line), which operated passenger and cargo steamers from both Boston and Providence to Philadelphia. That same day Morse bought the New York and Porto Rico Line. A month later the New Haven acquired a fifty per-cent interest and therefore virtual control of the Merchants and Miners Steamship Company, one of the largest and most profitable shipping companies along the Atlantic Coast. Merchants and Miners covered several coastal routes with vessels designed for both passengers and cargo, but their primary route, one which might have been especially valuable to Morse, was from Boston to Norfolk and Baltimore. The New Haven then turned the Winsor Line operation over to Merchants and Miners.

The only major American steamship line along the Atlantic Coast that appeared to be remaining independent in 1907 was the Ocean Steamship Company, better known as the Savannah Line, which operated passenger and freight steamships from both Boston and New York to Savannah. When Morse noted that the New Haven Railroad did not seem to be making an offer for the Savannah Line, he did. He was surprised, however, when the Savannah Line directors, unlike any others he had approached, remained adamantly unimpressed with the inflated offer he proffered and answered that they did not want to sell their line. What Morse apparently did not know was that the Savannah Line was controlled by the Central of Georgia Railroad, which was in turn controlled by the Southern Railroad, and that the Southern Railroad was controlled by J. Pierpont Morgan.

The New Haven Railroad's most damaging thrust in its duel with Charles W. Morse in 1907 was its purchase of the Maine Steamship Company, the line operating passenger and cargo steamers between New York and Portland, Maine, and the line Morse had been most eager to acquire for his Eastern Steamship Company.

The New Haven Railroad did not bring the Maine Steamship Company into its primary marine subsidiary, the New England Navigation Company. In this same period the New Haven had also recently

Camden on the Penobscot River.

gained control of two other local marine properties: the Joy Line, which operated small steamers (most of them, as we have seen, second-hand steamers from the Maine Coast) between New York and Providence at low fares in competition with the Railroad's own more prestigious Providence Line; and the Hartford and New York Transportation Company, which operated small overnight steamers between these two cities. For some reason, probably because the administration of Theodore Roosevelt was beginning to ask the Railroad embarrassing questions about violations of the Sherman Anti-Trust Act, the New Haven chose to maintain the Hartford and New York Transportation Company as a secondary subsidiary and to place the three recently acquired properties, the Hartford Line, the Providence Joy Line, and the Maine Steamship Company's Portland Line together under this separate aegis.

Two of the four new steel steamers then under construction for Morse were delivered by their builders in June, 1907. Early in the month the trim and beautifully proportioned *Camden*, the first of the new sisterships for the Bangor Line, was delivered by the Bath Iron Works. As noted, *Camden*, like *Gover-*

nor Cobb, was propelled by triple-screw direct-acting Parsons turbine engines. Also like *Governor Cobb*, her hull and Main Deck sheathing were of steel. Although most of her route was in the open ocean, since she would also have to navigate in the shallow waters of the Penosbcot River, *Camden* had an extreme draft of only ten feet, as opposed to the fourteen-foot draft of *Governor Cobb*. Also, to keep the draft low, neither *Camden* nor her later sistership *Belfast* were equipped with double bottoms as the other new Eastern Steamship vessels had been.

Camden, although her power, capacity, and interior layout were similar, presented a very different outward appearance from *Governor Cobb*. Since their route included about twenty miles on the winding Penobscot River, *Camden* and *Belfast* were narrower than *Governor Cobb* but achieved similar capacity with greater length. These steamers were 332 feet in overall length, even longer than *Calvin Austin* or *Governor Dingley*. But their extreme beam of only fifty-four feet gave them an unusual length-to-breadth ratio of nearly six to one. With their narrow hulls and triple screws, these new Bangor steamers proved exceptionally maneuverable in the winding Penobscot.

Yale of Charles W. Morse's Metropolitan Line upbound in the East River, New York.

Harvard. (Steamship Historical Society Collection, University of Baltimore Library)

Many years later, when serving as her master, Captain Norman Strickland, who at one time or another had served as master of all of the last four big sidewheelers of the Fall River Line, claimed *Camden* was the most maneuverable steamer, and in every way the easiest to handle, he had ever commanded. Both of the new Bangor steamers were also considerably faster than any of the earlier steamers on this route. *Camden*, which clocked over nineteen knots on her trials, well over her design speed of sixteen knots, proved even faster than *Governor Cobb*. For some reason, perhaps related to *Camden*'s long narrow hull, even though their engines were virtually identical and even though *Camden* had greater speed, *Camden* and later also her sistership *Belfast* consumed less fuel and thus proved far less expensive to operate than *Governor Cobb*.

As had been the case on *Calvin Austin, Governor Dingley,* and *Governor Cobb*, the Dining Saloon aboard *Camden* was located on the Quarter Deck just aft of the Entrance Hall. With its rows of curtained windows on both sides, this attractive dining area provided passengers with pleasant views, especially as part of the route was along the picturesque Penobscot River during daylight hours.

As *Camden* was only the second turbine-powered steamer completed in the United States, and the first built in New England, her trials, like those earlier of *Governor Cobb*, attracted considerable interest. When she was first fired up at Bath to sail down the Kennebec and into the ocean for her trials, among the many interested guests aboard were John S. Hyde, the President of the Bath Iron Works; C. F. Bailey, from the Newport News Shipbuilding and Dry Dock Company; Professor Charles H. Peabody from the Massachusetts Institute of Technology; and several respresentatives from the United States Navy.

After one cruise up the Maine coast with members of the various Consolidated boards and a round trip to New York to bring a group of travelling Texas bankers to Boston (during which she beat *Governor Cobb*'s New York-Boston record by nearly one hour), *Camden* finally made her first run from Boston to Bangor on June 21, 1907. That season, pending the completion of *Belfast, City of Rockland* remained on the Boston-Bangor route with the new *Camden*. As *Camden*, however, was much faster, the line had to publish two separate schedules for its two steamers. Replaced on the Bangor Line, *City of Bangor* was sent to run opposite *Ransom B. Fuller* on the

Kennebec route.

Yale, Harvard, and *Camden* were not the only new steamers produced for Eastern Steamship in 1907. In that year Morse also brought out the new 126-foot *Boothbay* for the Bath-Boothbay Harbor route. Although an excellent small steamer, *Boothbay* proved too large for this route and therefore uneconomical to operate. Two years later she was transferred to one of Morse's commuter routes on Penobscot Bay.

The great event of June, 1907, however, was the delivery of Morse's *Yale* later in the month. *Yale's* trial run from New York to Boston on June 29 was an overwhelming success. Aboard for the occasion were C. W. Morse, Calvin Austin, and most of the members of the Board and the company executives of the Metropolitan Line or of other companies in Consolidated Steamship's roster, as well as representatives from Roach's yard, from W. and A. Fletcher, and from John Englis and Son. *Yale's* commander was S. F. Pike, who had previously been master of *Ransom B. Fuller.* During this trial trip Andrew Fletcher himself took charge of the engines.

As *Yale* steamed up Long Island Sound that June day, she was moving at a speed greater than any vessel had ever achieved in American waters. On this trial trip *Yale* had no difficulty maintaining her design speed of twenty-four miles per hour (or about twenty-one knots). In fact she averaged about twenty-one knots for the entire trip and completed the 337 miles from New York to Boston in less than fourteen hours, one hour less than the record established earlier by *Camden* and more than an hour less than her later schedule would call for. Her officers claimed that at times she had even reached a speed of twenty-four knots, a claim hard to credit. (The Cunard Line's *Mauretania,* which also made her debut that season, and which was to hold the trans-Atlantic speed record for the next twenty years, had a top speed of just over twenty-six knots.) In any event, for many years, Morse's *Yale* and *Harvard* were recognized as the fastest ships in American registry.

Amazingly, despite this speed, *Yale* produced virtually no vibration. On her trial trip to Boston, someone pointed out that some glasses that happened to be placed fairly close together on a serving table in the Dining Saloon, located almost directly over the propellers, were not even rattling.

That the turbine-driven triple-screw *Yale* was fast was not a surprise. She had been designed for speed. What was news when the swift *Yale* first

coursed up the Sound was her extraordinary beauty. Both *Yale* and *Harvard,* with their long white hulls, their two strong raked smokestacks, and their delicate sheer, were exceptionally handsome vessels.

Morse's *Yale* was in every sense a magnificent steamship. Not quite so large as the Fall River Line's *Priscilla* or *Puritan,* at 407 feet in overall length she was nevertheless in the same league. *Yale* and *Harvard,* in some respects, seemed designed to appeal to a new and perhaps more descriminating traveller than the larger Long Island Sound steamers. Among *Priscilla's* 345 staterooms, for instance, just fifteen were larger rooms with beds rather than double-deck berths, and only one of these provided an adjoining private bathroom. Of *Yale's* 311 staterooms, on the other hand, forty had either twin beds or a large double bed rather than double-deck berths, and of these twenty-eight had adjoining bathrooms.

Yale's interior was attractive but, alas, not exceptional, as it essentially followed the typical pattern of the overnight steamers of the era. The dominant color throughout (carpets, curtains, etc.), one need hardly point out, was blue, and on *Harvard,* when she was ready, red. One innovation on these steamers was an attractive Smoking Room standing alone on the Hurricane Deck and surrounded by stained-glass windows. To create an effect roughly like that of a European Pub, the whole room was finished in oak, and lanterns hung from the ceiling over each table.

While *Yale's* progress up the Sound may have been smooth for her passengers, even when she was underway at high speed, the ride for vessels unfortunate enough to be caught in her wake, apparently, was not always smooth, if this contemporary news item is to be believed:

> A sea from the wake of the turbine steamer Yale boarded the ferryboat Chautauqua in the North River on Saturday and made a clean sweep of the lower deck, wetting everybody on the deck. It is said that the wave covered the deck to a depth of two feet.[4]

Although *Yale's* first trip to Boston had been successful beyond expectations, Charles W. Morse was reluctant to start his new Metropolitan Line passenger service to Boston until both steamers were ready, and in June, 1907, *Harvard* was still a long way from completion. For most of the season of 1907, *Yale* was assigned to take *Governor Cobb*'s place making the three round-trip direct runs to St. John on the International Line, while *Calvin Austin* made the stops at Eastport and Lubec. That season, therefore, found *Governor Cobb* running opposite *Governor Dingley* on the Portland Line. (In a sense, therefore, one could conceivably claim the incredible anomaly that *Yale* had replaced *St. Croix*.) Anyone assuming that *Yale* was far too large for the demands of the International Line (which, after all had been served by the small sidewheelers *Cumberland* and *State of Maine* only five years before) might note that many of *Yale*'s sailings to St. John that summer were fully booked.

In waiting until both of his new steamers had been completed before inaugurating his new passenger line between New York and Boston, Morse had to sacrifice the revenues of almost an entire season, for *Harvard* did not come from Fletcher's until September. The Metropolitan Line's new passenger service was finally inaugurated on September 16, 1907, with *Harvard* sailing from New York and *Yale* from Boston. Once in service these two smart and speedy steamers were immediately popular. They were not only fast, they proved good sea boats as well and were apparently able to meet their strenuous schedules regardless of weather or fog, even though they needed to steam at an average speed of over twenty miles per hour for the entire trip to do so.

The fact that *Yale* or *Harvard* could sail from Manhattan each evening at 5:00, just half an hour before the departure of the great Fall River Line steamers, and dock in Boston at 8:00 the following morning, at the same hour that the Fall River Line's Boston-bound passengers were arriving by train, had the expected effect of waving a very bright red flag in the face of J. Pierpont Morgan. In other words, the very success of his new liners was leading Charles W. Morse into serious trouble.

On September 21, just five days after *Yale* and *Harvard* started running to Boston, *Princeton*, the second large new steel-hulled sidewheel steamer for Morse's Albany night line, was launched. When completed, the 440-foot *Princeton* was expected to become the running mate of the similar *C. W. Morse*. At this time Morse also had two steel-hulled sisterships, somewhat smaller versions of *Princeton* and *C. W. Morse*, under construction for his line between New York and Troy.

By September of 1907 Charles Wyman Morse had reached the pinnacle of success. Only six years after he had entered the steamship business by purchasing the night line operating two small wooden-hulled sidewheelers between Boston and landings on the Kennebec River, Morse sat at the head of a vast shipping empire—the various lines comprising his Consolidated Steamship Company—operating in aggregate nearly one hundred vessels. He was actively replacing the older wooden-hulled sidewheelers of his Maine Coast lines with modern, steel-hulled propeller-driven steamers; he had added one large steel-hulled sidewheel steamer to his Hudson River lines and had three more under construction; his innovative *Yale* and *Harvard* for the new passenger service between New York and Boston had proved successful beyond all expectations; and in addition he controlled a fleet of ocean-going steamships sailing regularly out of New York or Boston for Puerto Rico, Cuba, Florida, and Texas.

1. John Haskell Kemble, "Harvard and Yale," <u>Steamboat Bill</u>, VII (April, 1942), pp. 102-3.
2. John M. Richardson, <u>Steamboat Lore of the Penobscot</u>, Augusta, 1941, pp. 33-40.
3. Quoted in <u>Nautical Gazette</u>, May 3, 1906, p. 331.
4. <u>Nautical Gazette</u>, Oct. 31, 1907, p. 294.

III. Götterdämmerung: 1907-1910

Within only a few days after Morse's unprecedented success in the marine world had been crowned with the inauguration of his new passenger service to Boston with two of the finest ships in America, events occured which were to bring his vast shipping empire crashing around him. In October, 1907, as a result of a relatively minor market slump, one of the New York banks in which Morse was involved was unable to meet its obligations and was forced to go out of business. When its depositors found that they had lost a great deal of money, apparently as a result of the bank's mismanagement, a government investigation ensued. What federal examiners discovered was that the percentage of the bank's assets invested in a single enterprise, namely the Consolidated Steamship Company controlled by Morse, who was one of the bank's directors, had far exceeded the amount allowed by federal banking laws. They also discovered that the ledgers of this bank, and also of other banks in which Morse had influence, had been fraudulently manipulated in an effort to hide this fact.

Since Morse himself and his various companies were among the depositors of this and other banks whose assets had been lost or sequestered, the Metropolitan Line was now unable either to make payments due on the construction of *Yale* and *Harvard* or to cover the interest due on its enormous bond issue. As a result, Morse's creditors were able to place liens on his two new Metropolitan Line steamers.

Shortly after the results of the government investigations were published, Charles Wyman Morse and his wife suddenly realized that the fall of 1907 had become an ideal time to enjoy the cultural advantages of a tour of Europe. Back in Boston, Calvin Austin found that he had been left to deal with the burden which had unexpectedly dropped on the Metropolitan Line as well as he could by himself.

With Morse far away in Europe, a group of Metropolitan Line stockholders, in an effort to save their enormous investments while *Yale* and *Harvard* were still in their own hands, approached Charles Mellen and asked whether the New Haven Railroad might be interested in buying the New York-to-Boston service of the Metropolitan Line. Mellen refused. In what seems in retrospect, given later events, poor judgment, Mellen (or more likely, Morgan) took the position that the consistent policy of the New Haven was to give full support to its own Fall River Line, in which the Railroad had a very substantial investment. Any successful passenger and cargo line running directly between New York and Boston, whether operated by others or by the New Haven itself, would take traffic away from the Fall River Line. Mellen's primary objective, therefore, was to make sure there was no steamer line running from New York to Boston. Were he to buy the line, even at the minimal price being offered, Metropolitan's other stockholders might be able to prevent him from cancelling the service. If he did not buy it, however, it appeared that a combination of the company's creditors and the federal government was about to put the line out of business for him.

Mellen was in something of a quandry, however, now that the future of the Metropolitan Line was looking daily more dubious, in deciding what to do with the three fast freighters in the construction of which the railroad had invested several million dollars. These large freight steamers had been built solely for the purpose of forcing the Metropolitan Line out of business. Now that it appeared the Metropolitan was about to go under without their help, Mellen had no other suitable service for them. After these freighters had been completed and delivered during the summer of 1907, they had been employed occasionally on cargo runs to Fall River, where they had shown that, while they were not so fast as *Yale* or *Harvard*, they were capable of considerable speed. For the most part, however, these three steamers had remained idle in lay-up waiting to see how events would affect the Metropolitan Line. Finally, in January 1908, probably because Mellen already had contracts with Boston merchants due to take effect on the first of the year, the New Haven's fast freighters, *Massachusetts*, *Bunker Hill*, and *Old Colony*, operating as the Boston Merchants Line, a division of the railroad's New England Navigation Company, began plying between New

Bunker Hill leaving New York about 1908. When Morse placed his passenger steamers, *Yale* and *Harvard*, on the Metropolitan Line, the New England Navigation Company competed with the three fast sisterships, *Bunker Hill*, *Massachusetts*, and *Old Colony*, which appeared at first as freighters, as shown here. (Steamship Historical Society Collection, University of Baltimore Library)

York and Boston. Since the Boston Merchants Line at first scheduled only three sailings a week from each port, it would seem that one of these fast freighters could probably have handled the route alone.

Yale and *Harvard* were not in operation at this time of year, and the Metropolitan Line was sending out only its older freight steamers. With their deliberately lower rates (25% below the published rates of the Metropolitan Line), the New Haven's fast freighters, of course, operated at a considerable loss. Although it was never stated in writing, the objective of the New Haven, which could afford to absorb the loss (or at least believed it could) was to keep running these freighters only as long as was needed for the low rates to drain the freight revenues of the Metropolitan Line and force it out of business. Apparently the New Haven's ploy nearly succeeded, for Calvin Austin later admitted that once the Merchant Line's freight service between New York and Boston started, Metropolitan's freight revenues dropped alarmingly.

On February 4, 1908, Morse's Consolidated Steamship Company, which had been unable to make its enormous interest payments for several months,

declared bankruptcy, and a few weeks later the conglomerate was simply dissolved. Miraculously, although many of the stockholders had been forced to absorb personal losses, all of Consolidated's constituent companies were able to extracate themselves from the ruins and again to operate independently.

The Hudson Navigation Company, still owned by Morse, remained solvent. The company was even in a position to continue the construction of *Trojan* and *Rensselaer*, the two new steamers for the Troy Line. Work was halted indefinitely, however, on *Princeton*, the much larger new steamer under construction for the Albany night line. (When this magnificent steamer, the largest steamboat ever operated regularly on the Hudson River, was finally completed in 1913, six years later, her collegiate name, which seemed to associate her too closely with the discredited Metropolitan Line, was given up, and she joined the line as *Berkshire*.)

The four steamship companies operating southward into the Atlantic out of New York—New York and Puerto Rico, New York and Cuba Mail, Clyde, and Mallory—all resurfaced as independent concerns.

Governor Dingley leaving Eastport, Maine, after she had been transferred to the International Division in 1910. (R. Loren Graham Collection, Steamship Historical Society, University of Baltimore Library)

They did, however, join in a relatively loose umbrella organization called the Atlantic, Gulf, and West Indies Steamship Company (or AGWI for short). This system allowed the component companies considerable freedom but also gave them the advantages of mutual co-operation.

After being placed in the hands of receivers, both the Eastern Steamship Company and the Metropolitan Steamship Company also managed to survive and to continue operating after rather thorough re-organizations in both cases. Both, however, were hampered by the enormous bond debts they carried. After the re-organizations Calvin Austin again emerged as President of both Eastern and Metropolitan. In the process of reconstructing the finances of the Eastern Steamship Company, now that Charles W. Morse was no longer to be associated with it, Calvin Austin sought the services of Hayden, Stone, and Company, a respected Boston investment firm. From this time both Josiah Hayden, as Chairman of the Board, and Galen Stone, as Treasurer of the Company, became closely associated with Calvin Austin in the management of the Eastern Steamship Company.

In March, 1908, Charles Wyman Morse, who by then had been persuaded that a return to the United States might be in his better interests, was indicted on federal charges of fraud, and his trial was set for October.

As soon as the warmer weather returned about mid-April, the glamorous *Yale* and *Harvard*, in spite of the financial and legal problems hovering over their operation, began their first full season on the Metropolitan Line's New York-to-Boston route. Again, they were immensely popular, again they sailed well-booked on every trip, but again the company, with steamers expensive to operate and burdened with interest payments, was not making much of a profit. A serious problem for the Metropolitan Line was that *Yale* and *Harvard* were expensive to operate and could therefore earn a profit only if they sailed virtually fully booked every night. During the summer season they usually did sail fully booked. But as the cooler weather approached traffic declined, so that Metropolitan had to cancel its passenger service to Boston every year from the end of November to about mid-April. During these months the Boston route was served again only by the four Metropolitan Line freighters. Unfortunately, by running for only about eight months a year, the coal-hungry *Yale* and *Harvard* barely paid for their own operation let alone for interest on bonds. Morse had at first scouted about in an effort to find a suitable winter run for his new steamers and had given serious thought to operating them between New York and Havana on his New York and Cuba Mail Line during the winter. By 1908, however, Morse no longer controlled the line to Havana.

The 1908 season was the first in which the New York-Boston route was served by two lines, the Metropolitan Line's fast passenger and cargo steamers *Yale* and *Harvard* and the New Haven Railroad's Boston Merchants Line with its freight steamers *Bunker Hill* and *Massachusetts*, which had also been built for speed. On one occasion *Bunker Hill* emerged from Tietjen and Lange's repair yards on the New Jersey side of the Hudson and headed for Fall River just as *Harvard* was leaving her pier en route to Boston. Once in the open part of the Sound past Sands Point, a signal from *Bunker Hill* suggested a race. With *Bunker Hill* running light—in this case with no cargo at all—and *Harvard* not only carrying a full load of cargo but also with her officers responsible for the safety of about a thousand passengers, *Bunker Hill* was able to claim a victory when she reached Point Judith about ten minutes ahead of *Harvard*. On another occasion, however, when *Bunker Hill* was carrying a full load, and an unofficial race was declared in the early morning when the two fast steamers were headed toward New York, *Harvard* easily took and maintained a lead. Given statistics derived from relative power or from builders' trials rather than races on the Sound, there is no question that *Yale* and *Harvard* were the faster ships. Although the New Haven's large freight steamers, *Bunker Hill* and *Massachusetts*, were demonstrably not quite as fast as *Yale* and *Harvard*, one should note that, with similar tonnage but only three-quarters the horsepower, they were nevertheless almost as fast. Morse had believed he had to turn to British naval architects to design the hulls for his new steamers. But as the hulls of New Haven's Boston steamers had been designed by their own engineers, these people, probably in this case primarily Stevenson Taylor, deserve considerable credit.

In the Eastern Steamship operation in 1908, *Camden*, rather than *Yale*, served on the International Line with *Calvin Austin* and *Governor Cobb*. During her previous season, *Camden*'s first on the Bangor Line, it seems that some of the aging wooden wharves along the Penobscot had not proved strong enough to take

the daily thrusts of this powerful steel-hulled propeller steamer as she came alongside for her early morning landings. So for the 1908 season, the gentler wooden-hulled sidewheelers, *City of Bangor* and *City of Rockland* (which were much easier to control in a quick landing operation) were again together on the Bangor Line while the piers were being strengthened. And, as *Governor Cobb* also returned to the International Line that season, *Bay State* was back on the Portland Line with *Governor Dingley*. Meanwhile, *Penobscot* returned to the Kennebec Line to run opposite *Ransom B. Fuller*.

The work on *Belfast*, the second of the new sisterships for the Bangor route, had been halted for several months when the company first realized that its finances were locked up, and that it had no way to continue payments to the shipyard. By the summer of 1908, however, once the Eastern Steamship Company had been re-organized, Austin was able to ask the Bath Iron Works to resume construction of *Belfast*. Delivery was promised in time for the season of 1909.

The trial of Charles W. Morse began in New York on October 14, 1908. Three weeks later, on November 6, Morse was convicted on several charges of fraud with intent to deceive and sentenced to fifteen years in the federal prison in Atlanta. Pending an appeal, which his lawyers filed immediately, Morse was placed in "The Tombs," the local prison in lower Manhattan, from where, in typical Morse style, he continued to manage his businesses and to receive and deal with associates as though his cell were an office. When on January 17, 1909, Morse was released on bail, he simply returned to a full work schedule until the appeal trial began.

Through the season of 1909 *Yale* and *Harvard* again provided the New York-to-Boston service of the Metropolitan Line. These steamers still had the support of the public and still sailed fully booked on virtually every trip, but the combination of the cost of operating these fast steamers, the line's heavy debt, and the continuing efforts of Morgan, Mellen, and the New Haven Railroad to undermine the company still kept the financial future of the Metropolitan Line in constant doubt.

Early in 1909 *Belfast* was completed at Bath, so that this became the first season in which the handsome sisterships, *Belfast* and *Camden*, ran together on Eastern's Boston-Bangor route. These fast triple-screw turbine-driven steamers were able to cut more than two hours from the Boston-to-Bangor schedule previously maintained by *City of Bangor* and *City of Rockland*.

With *Belfast* and *Camden* now running to Bangor, the near sisterships, *City of Rockland* and *City of Bangor*, were now both transferred to Eastern's Kennebec Line, in the process releasing the relatively new *Ransom B. Fuller* and the older *Penobscot*, which had previously covered this route. *Penobscot*, according to some sources, had been sold to the New Haven Railroad's low-fare Joy Line on Long Island Sound at the end of the 1908 season, presumably to replace that line's lost *Larchmont* (formerly *Cumberland* of the International Line), but there is no record of *Penobscot's* having operated on the Joy Line in 1908 or 1909. In any event, she was later sold to McAllister Brothers of New York. Between 1910 and 1915 *Penobscot*, renamed *Mohawk* in 1912, operated on a low-fare line between New York and Albany on the Hudson River (on which her running mate was *Kennebec*, in 1912 renamed *Iroquois*) in opposition to Morse's Albany night line. During the First World War *Penobscot* was partially dismantled and her hull converted into a sailing vessel which, after its first departure from New York, was never heard from again.

For the season of 1909 *Ransom B. Fuller*, the last wooden-hulled sidewheeler built for a Maine Coast overnight service, was placed on the International Division with *Calvin Austin* and *Governor Cobb*. By the time the season of 1910 started, however, someone at Eastern had finally figured out that the three modern steel propeller steamers, *Calvin Austin*, *Governor Dingley*, and *Governor Cobb* belonged together on the long ocean route of the International Division, an arrangement these steamers maintained until the service was interrupted by the First World War. With *Governor Dingley* now running to St. John, *Ransom B. Fuller*, with belated logic, was assigned to the shorter Boston-Portland route with *Bay State*.

Apparently the Portland Line in 1909 was enjoying a last spate of extraordinarily heavy traffic before automobiles and trucks decreed its hasty decline. During the winter of 1909-1910, in order to maximize their stateroom capacity, both *Ransom B. Fuller* and *Bay State* were barbarized. *Ransom B. Fuller*, a very handsome steamer, and *Bay State*, which was also attractive, were apparently placed in the hands of some aesthetic Philistine to emerge as two egregiously ungainly, though admittedly capacious, steamboats before starting their service on the Port-

land Line for the season of 1910. *Bay State* was dismantled down to the guards. In the one advantageous aspect of her rebuilding, her big sidewheels were replaced by smaller feathering wheels, like those with which *Ransom B. Fuller* had been equipped when she was built. Then above the guards a whole new steamer was constructed, with two full decks of staterooms and a row of staterooms on a Dome Deck above that. The large Fall River Line steamers could carry a Dome Deck of that sort gracefully. But *Bay State* was less than 300 feet in length and, for the sake of relatively few extra rooms, this height simply made her appear stubby and topheavy. If increased capacity to accommodate the burgeoning traffic to Portland was the only object of this unfortunate transformation, then the object was achieved, for the rebuilt *Bay State* carried 245 staterooms, even more than *Calvin Austin*, as opposed to the 163 staterooms she had carried when she was built in 1895.

The treatment of *Ransom B. Fuller* was even more unfortunate. The handsome little steamer was cut in two somewhere forward of her smokestack, and a forty-five-foot section added between the two parts. In the process the number of her staterooms was increased from 173 to an incredible 265. The operation might still have resulted in a reasonably handsome steamer, except that, since the addition was forward of her smokestack, her single stack was now not only aft of center but also on top of a new row of staterooms added too far aft on her Dome Deck. As a result *Ransom B. Fuller's* profile had been thrown out of proportion, giving the steamer an unpleasantly awkward appearance.

In spite of all of the problems facing the Metropolitan Line, in 1910 *Yale* and *Harvard* were ready to start their third full season on the New York-to-Boston route. Before opening this season, both of these steamers had been converted from coal-burning to oil-burning in an effort to decrease, if possible, their high operating costs. By this time also their owners had begun playing a complicated game of creating new corporate entities presumably to prevent these two steamers from being taken over by the creditors who still held a lien on them. Thus in 1910 the original Metropolitan Steamship Company registered in Maine sold *Yale* and *Harvard*, as well as the four Metropolitan Line freighters, to another Metropolitan Steamship Company (with the same stockholders and the same officers but not liable for the original company's debts) registered in New Jersey. Mean-

Ransom B. Fuller in Boston Harbor before her lengthening in 1909.
(Steamship Historical Society Collection, University of Baltimore Library)

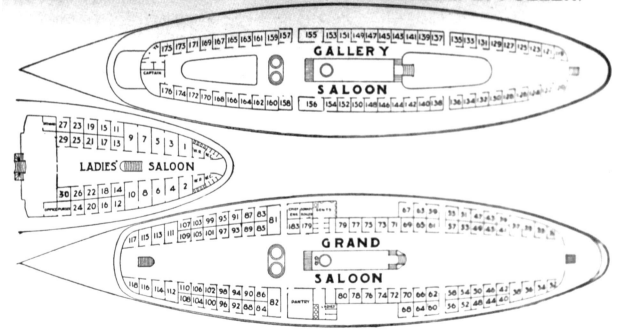

Deck plans of *Ransom B. Fuller* before her lengthening.

Ransom B. Fuller in Boston Harbor after her lengthening.

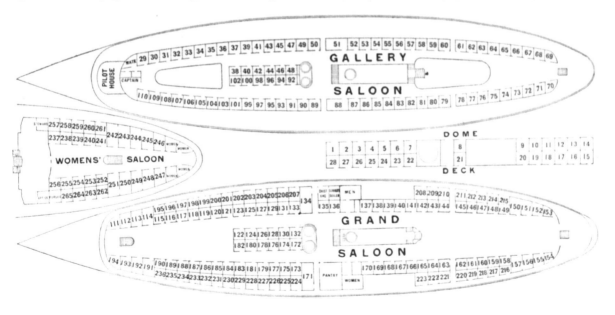

Deck plans of *Ransom B. Fuller* after her lengthening.

Bay State before she was rebuilt in 1909.

Bay State after she was rebuilt in 1909.

while the New Haven Railroad, which had apparently changed its mind about wanting to become associated with the Metropolitan Line, helped salvage the original Metropolitan Steamship Company (of Maine) by buying sufficient stock both to be able to exercise some control over the company and to repurchase the four freighters (on which there were no liens) from the New Jersey Metropolitan Steamship Company. This original Metropolitan Steamship Company (Maine) also apparently continued to operate *Yale* and *Harvard* during the 1910 season by chartering them from the New Jersey version of the Metropolitan Steamship Company.

Since the New Haven Railroad had, it seems, decided to accept the fact that it could safely play a role in the affairs of the Metropolitan Steamship Company (of Maine, in case anyone has lost track), it really no longer needed to maintain a line of its own on this route. In March, 1910, therefore, Mellen gave up the service of the Boston Merchants Line after only two years of operation, and the large freighters *Massachusetts*, *Bunker Hill*, and *Old Colony*, so recently constructed for the New Haven at great cost, were again relegated to lay-up. Needless to say, the Boston merchants who had been supporting the railroad's freight service to Boston to take advantage of its lower rates, now had to pay full rates to the railroad-controlled Metropolitan Line.

The season of 1910 was the last for the beautiful *Yale* and *Harvard* on the New York-Boston route. If this route were to be maintained, there could be no vessels better suited for it than *Yale* and *Harvard*. But as long as the Metropolitan Line held ownership of these primary assets of the company (or companies?), the threat remained that its creditors might at any time be able to take possession of them. Thus the surest way for the stockholders to protect their investment was to unload these vulnerable material assets in exchange for as much cash as possible. As they no doubt already suspected, the Metropolitan stockholders found that the New Haven Railroad stood ready to assist them in doing so.

During the summer of 1910 an arrangement was worked out according to which the Pacific Coast Navigation Company would lease (and later buy, thus enabling Metropolitan to pay off the debts and release the lien) *Yale* and *Harvard* for a new overnight line between San Francisco and San Pedro (the port for Los Angeles). Their season on the Boston route was cut short at the end of September, 1910, and *Yale* and *Harvard* were readied for their long journey to the West Coast. Only a few days later the pair headed southward down the Atlantic and around Cape Horn. As fuel oil was then not always available at some of the South American ports along the way, the engines of the two steamers were re-converted to burn coal before they left.

Yale and *Harvard*, as it turned out, were even more ideally suited for their new assignment in California than they had been for the New York-to-Boston route. With their extraordinary speed, these two ships could, by steaming out of San Francisco in the late afternoon and arriving in San Pedro during the following morning, manage this long distance as an overnight run, which few if any other American steamships at that time could have done.

Yale and *Harvard* long remained popular on the California coast. During the First World War, both were taken across the Atlantic to serve as transports in the English Channel for the duration of the conflict, but when the war ended they returned to California and, after a rather thorough refurbishing, were back on the San Francisco-San Pedro run, which soon afterward was extended to San Diego. After *Harvard* was lost by running hard on the rocks at Point Arguello in 1931, Clyde-Mallory Line's *Iroquois* (1927) was chartered to take her place for one season. When even this fairly new vessel proved unable to maintain the line's demanding schedule, however, *Yale* handled the route alone for four more years until the Depression and a series of strikes ended the service in 1936. *Yale* survived to serve as a barracks ship during World War II, appropriately renamed *Greyhound*, but she was finally scrapped in 1947, by which time she had been in service for forty years.

By the time *Yale* and *Harvard*, the ships in which he had taken such personal pride, steamed away from New England, Morse had lost his appeal trial and had started his fifteen-year sentence in the federal prison in Atlanta. The Eastern Steamship Company and the Metropolitan Steamship Company were left in the competent hands of Calvin Austin, although both companies, still carrying the huge debts amassed by Morse, were in perilous financial condition.

Harvard at her wharf in Los Angeles (San Francisco Maritime National Historic Park, Randolph Brandt Photographic Collection)

IV. Corporate Roulette: 1910-1923

Soon after *Yale* and *Harvard* had steamed off together to the west coast, Charles Mellen, President of the New Haven Railroad, in a tone of condescending largesse, announced to the people of Boston that the New Haven Railroad would undertake to continue the passenger service between New York and Boston in succeeding seasons by converting their three fast freighters into passenger steamers and placing them on the route between New York and Boston previously served by *Yale* and *Harvard*. These steamers had been owned by the New Haven Railroad's primary marine subsidiary, the New England Navigation Company, which by 1910 had been re-organized as the New England Steamship Company. For reasons best understood by himself or perhaps only by his lawyers, Mellen did not want the New England Steamship Company to operate the planned passenger line to Boston. The New England Steamship Company, therefore, "sold" the three freighters to the Maine Steamship Company (the New York-to-Portland line), which was itself part of the Hartford and New York Transportation Company, the second marine subsidiary of the New Haven Railroad. Thus it was the Maine Steamship Company which was to rebuild the three freighters as passenger steamers (with money "borrowed" from the New England Steamship Company!) and to run them between New York and Boston calling the route the "Metropolitan Line," although the Maine Steamship Company was not in any way a part of either of the New Jersey version (now defunct) or the Maine version (still alive) of the Metropolitan Steamship Company.

Since the New Haven Railroad, in its generosity to the people travelling between New York and Boston, was apparently prepared to spend a great deal of money converting its three fast freighters to serve as both passenger and cargo vessels, one has to wonder why the Railroad could not have used the same outlay to purchase *Yale* and *Harvard*, steamers whose popularity on the New York-Boston run had already been demonstrated and which had already earned themselves a host of devoted followers. By purchasing *Yale* and *Harvard* from the Metropolitan Line and

operating these steamers themselves, the New Haven could have provided Metropolitan with the cash to pay its debts and thus lift the liens on the steamers. All parties would have been ahead financially, and the Railroad would have had a far better set of steamers for the New York-Boston service it had inherited than the ones they were rebuilding. Undoubtedly Mr. Mellen's lawyers had reasons which may now never be known.

During the winter of 1910-1911 *Massachusetts*, *Bunker Hill*, and *Old Colony* were stripped to their hulls and completely rebuilt from the guards up as passenger vessels (still with considerable space for cargo on their Main Decks, nevertheless). Apparently the new design was not provided by the naval architect who had been responsible for rebuilding *Bay State* and *Ransom B. Fuller*, for after the conversion these three vessels emerged as reasonably attractive passenger steamers, although perhaps the word "substantial" might be more appropriate. On the other hand, they did not even minimally approach the beautiful lines of *Yale* and *Harvard*, the ships they were designed to replace.

For some tastes the interiors of these three steamers, however, might have been considered more attractive than those of *Yale* and *Harvard*. *Yale* and *Harvard*, while racy and modern on the exterior, had, as mentioned, rather conservative interiors in a somewhat heavy style which might be called a muted Victorian. The interiors of *Massachusetts*, *Bunker Hill*, and *Old Colony*, on the other hand, were rather simple, but therefore also bright, with unadorned walls painted a light ivory and banisters of polished wood, in a style that was to become popular in the 1920s. Whether this decor was chosen because it was more modern or because it was both cheaper and faster to execute is now hard to determine. Particularly attractive on these steamers were their Dining Saloons. Located high on their Gallery Decks forward, the dining areas were surrounded by windows, which not only rendered them light and cheerful but also provided passengers with a clear view of passing scenery. Aft of the Dining Saloons on the port side on

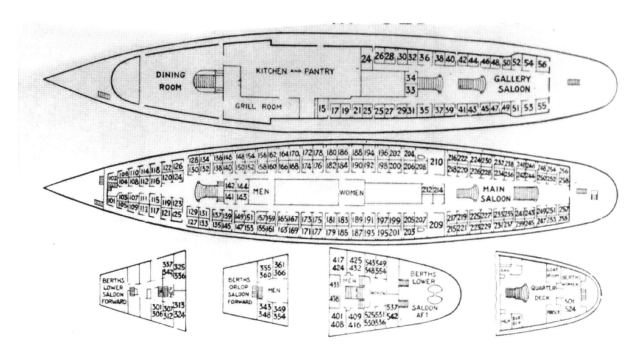

Stateroom plans of *Massachusetts*, *Bunker Hill*, and *Old Colony* after passenger accommodations were added in 1911.

each of the steamers also was a handsomely panelled area called the "Grill Room," but which apparently served mainly as a bar.

For the season of 1911 *Bunker Hill* and *Massachusetts*, the two among the three powered by the more typical triple-expansion reciprocating engines, were placed on a New York-Boston overnight route advertised, as we have noted, as the "Metropolitan Line," but actually under the management of the Maine Steamship Company, a subsidiary of the Hartford and New York Transportation Company, which was itself a subsidiary of the New York, New Haven, and Hartford Railroad. The turbine-powered *Old Colony*, which was not needed on the New York-Boston route except as a spare in emergencies, was assigned to the Maine Steamship Company's original route between New York and Portland to augment the service provided by the company's former steamers, *North Land* of 1910 and *North Star* of 1901.

By the end of the 1911 season Mellen and the Board of the New Haven Railroad were obliged to learn what Morse must already have known: that operating large steamers with enough speed to cover the New York-to-Boston route around Cape Cod as an overnight run, and operating them for revenue for only half of the year, could barely produce a profit let alone amortize the cost of building these large steamers in

the first place.

Meanwhile, although all of the Maine Coast lines of the Eastern Steamship Company had been operating as usual, Calvin Austin was struggling to find ways to meet all of the debt obligations of the company while still maintaining its marginally profitable seasonal services. Apparently the company's finances had not been entirely depleted, for in 1911 Eastern produced two small steel-hulled propeller steamers, *Southport* and *Westport*, for its Bath-Boothbay Harbor line. With these attractive new steamers on the run in 1911, *Winter Harbor* was sold and *Island Belle* scrapped, though *Nahanada* and *Wiwurna* (both named for local Indian chiefs) remained on the route to assist the newer boats.

Late in December, 1911, Charles Mellen, Calvin Austin, Josiah Hayden, Galen Stone, and a group of lawyers got together and worked out a plan that was expected to be advantageous to all parties. First they created a new company called the Eastern Steamship Corporation, with Calvin Austin as President. This new concern took over all of the assets and properties of the former Eastern Steamship Company, which was thereupon dissolved. It also took over such assets as existed (and debts as well, of course) of the Metropolitan Steamship Company, thus bringing the Metropolitan Line for the first time into the same corpo-

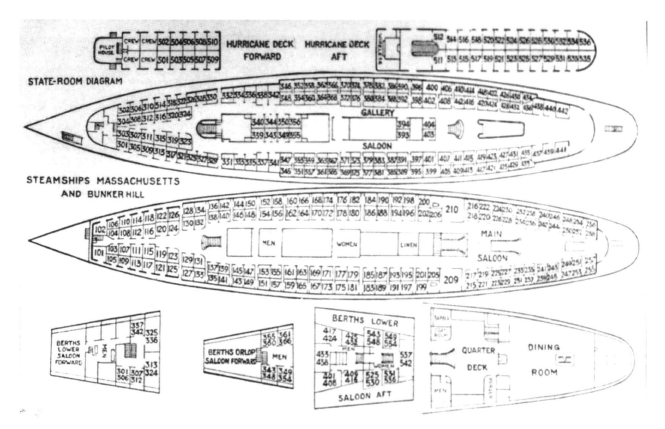

Stateroom plans of *Massachusetts* and *Bunker Hill* as modified in 1912. *Old Colony* was not altered at that time.

ration as the Maine Coast lines. In order to buttress the finances of this new Eastern Steamship Corporation, the New Haven Railroad turned over its profitable Maine Steamship Company, which included not only the New York-Portland Line with its steamers *Old Colony*, *North Land*, and *North Star*, but also the recently-converted New York-Boston liners, *Massachusetts* and *Bunker Hill*.

In return for this major contribution of marine properties, the New Haven Railroad was granted thirty per-cent of the shares of the new Eastern Steamship Corporation, making the Railroad Eastern's largest stockholder. The New Haven also provided the new company with a welcome financial infusion by purchasing over forty per-cent of its new bond issue.

Early in 1912, once financing had been arranged for the new corporation, *Massachusetts* and *Bunker Hill* (but not *Old Colony*) were returned to the shipyard for yet another major rebuilding to increase their passenger capacities significantly in the hope of making them somewhat more profitable. On each of these sisterships virtually the entire Gallery Deck was gutted, including, unfortunately, the Dining Saloons located far forward on this deck, which had

been one of the most attractive aspects of these steamers. The Dining Saloons were now placed aft on the Main Deck, but without windows, and double rows of staterooms on both sides of the steamer—virtually repeating the stateroom layout of the Saloon Deck below—were built the full length of their Gallery Decks. These additions plus a new row of staterooms on the Dome Deck above increased the total number of staterooms on *Massachusetts* and *Bunker Hill* from 206 (fewer in fact than on the much smaller *Calvin Austin*, *Bay State*, or *Ransom B. Fuller*) to 336 or only minimally fewer than on the Fall River Line's larger *Priscilla*.

For the season of 1912 *Bunker Hill* and *Massachusetts*, with over a hundred new staterooms to bolster their passenger capacity, returned to the New York-Boston route, which was now a part of the Eastern Steamship Corporation. In the company's ads and brochures, however, its New York-Boston service was still called the "Metropolitan Line," though the Metropolitan Steamship Company no longer existed.

In 1912 the Eastern Steamship Corporation added a new line to its list of services when it purchased the Boston and Yarmouth Steamship Company.

Bunker Hill, as she appeared after 1912.

This line, previously a Canadian-owned company, operated the two sisterships, *Prince George* of 1898 and *Prince Arthur* of 1899 (named for the two sons of King Edward VII, one of whom had in 1910 become King George V), both of British registry. These rakish two-stacked steamers, each just under three hundred feet in overall length, were clearly British in style and did not at all resemble Eastern's Maine Coast steamers. A third steamer, *Boston*, acquired from an earlier line on the route that the Boston and Yarmouth Steamship Company had bought out, served mostly as a spare. Since *Old Colony* and *North Land* sufficed to provide the New York-Portland route's scheduled three sailings per week from each port, the New York-Portland line's third steamer, *North Star*, which was larger than *Prince George* or *Prince Arthur*, was now frequently assigned to the Yarmouth route during the summer months.

The new Eastern Steamship Corporation, although competently managed, was obliged to function with two strong liabilities: One was the tremendous debt it had inherited from Charles W. Morse. The other was the fact that virtually all of its passenger services were seasonal, earning profitable revenues

for only a few months of the year, while their ships and other properties had to be maintained and their interest payments had to be raised for all twelve months of the year.

It was also during the year 1912 that Charles W. Morse, then in his second year in the federal prison in Atlanta, managed, by forcing into his stomach a concoction of unattractive substances he had been told would serve his purpose, to convince the prison doctor that he was dying of a fatal disease. When a sympathetic President Taft thereupon granted him a pardon, Morse returned home, where he was soon miraculously cured of his "fatal disease." Although there is no evidence that Morse ever again participated in the affairs of Eastern Steamship, he did return to an active management of his Hudson River lines for the rest of his life and became involved in a variety of other marine-oriented ventures.

Somehow the new Eastern Steamship Corporation managed to remain solvent through the seasons of 1912 and 1913, which were boom years for all American steamship companies. In 1914, however, the company was unable to make its interest payments and was forced to declare bankruptcy.

Massachusetts, as she appeared after 1912, about to pass under the Brooklyn Bridge upbound in the East River on her way to Boston.

When Calvin Austin turned to the New Haven Railroad, which still owned nearly one-third of Eastern Steamship, for help, he found that the railroad too was experiencing serious financial difficulties of its own.

In 1913 the Interstate Commerce Commission, stung into action by revelations of the New Haven's incompetence by the young lawyer, Louis Brandeis, and recently invigorated by new and stronger anti-trust legislation passed by Congress that year, had initiated an investigation into the affairs of the New Haven Railroad and its complex system of subsidiaries. This probe eventually revealed—as almost any casual observer probably could have told them—that in its policy of creating a monopoly of New England transportation systems at any cost, and in the process buying up one potential competitor after another or starting new companies of its own to force competitors out of business, the Railroad had incurred a debt so great (over $65,000,000) that it could be construed as a criminal abuse of its investors' trust.

Since the great J. Pierpont Morgan had conveniently died in 1913, the blame for the New Haven's mismanagement fell on Charles Mellen, who had probably been responsible only for implementing Morgan's seemingly insatiable expansionist policies. As a result the New Haven was also forced to declare bankruptcy in 1914—a serious blow to all small investors of New England who had believed New Haven Railroad stock was the one sure asset they could count on—and Mr. Mellen was obliged to resign in disgrace.

In the wake of its investigation, the federal government made it clear to the New Haven that to avoid further anti-trust action the railroad would have to divest itself of all holdings in the Eastern Steamship Corporation. In order to comply with this government directive as quickly as possible, the New Haven sold its Eastern stocks and bonds in 1914, much of it to the other Eastern Steamship stockholders, at prices well below their par value. Considering the three large freight steamers the railroad had built in 1907 and then recently converted into passenger carriers at great expense, the Maine Steamship Company with its two fairly new vessels which it had turned over to Eastern, and its large financial investment in Eastern Steamship stocks and bonds of only two years before, in giving up its holdings in Eastern, the railroad suffered an enormous loss at a time when it was already in financial difficulty. Furthermore, the all-water over-

Prince George: The sisterships *Prince George* and *Prince Arthur* served on the Boston-Yarmouth route acquired by Eastern Steamship in 1912.
(R. Loren Graham Collection, Steamship Historical Society, University of Baltimore Library)

night steamer line between New York and Boston, which the New Haven had considered a serious threat to its own Fall River Line even when the railroad managed the line itself, was now in the hands of a completely independent competing steamship company.

Separated from the New Haven Railroad, but still in bankruptcy, Eastern Steamship was again placed under the control of a receiver, but in this case Calvin Austin, the company's President, was assigned that duty, in which he still had the advice and assistance of Hayden, Stone, and Company.

The last week of June, 1914, saw the start of the First World War in Europe. During the summer, therefore, the British government requisitioned *Prince George* and *Prince Arthur*, the two steamers serving on Eastern's Boston-Yarmouth route, which were still in British registry. As a result Eastern had to maintain only a curtailed service on the Yarmouth Line with *North Star* for the duration of the war.

The one positive event for the Eastern Steamship Corporation in 1914 was the opening of the Cape Cod Canal on 29 July, although Eastern's steamers did not start using the canal until the season of 1916 by which time canal had been somewhat more thor-

oughly dredged. By using the route through this canal rather than steaming all the way around the Cape, the New York-to-Boston steamers could reduce their run from 337 miles to 264 miles. Considering that the average cruising speed of *Massachusetts* and *Bunker Hill* was about twenty miles per hour, the new route through the canal should have cut about four hours from the trip. In practice, however, the saving in time could not be so great. In its early years, the Cape Cod Canal had several turns and in places was only about 100 feet in width. Also, while Buzzards Bay at the western entrance to the canal seems open and wide, the marked channel through its many rocks and shoals is in fact rather narrow. Consequently, even in fair weather steamers could make the canal passage only with caution and at reduced speed. In fog or foul weather steamers had to proceed even more cautiously and were often obliged to follow the former route through Nantucket Sound and around the Cape. Nevertheless, the Metropolitan Line steamers were able to cut one and a half hours from their schedule. Since they were no longer obliged to operate at full speed, the use of the canal also cut a considerable amount from the company's oil bills. Starting in the 1916

Bay State at her wharf in Boston.

Calvin Austin backing into her wharf at Boston.
(R. Loren Graham Collection, Steamship Historical Society, University of Baltimore Library)

season, Metropolitan Line steamers departed from either New York or Boston at 6:00 P.M. (one half hour later than the steamers of the Fall River Line) and were scheduled to arrive at the other end at 7:30 in the morning (one half hour before the Fall River Line's Boston passengers were due to arrive there by train).

Toward the end of the 1916 season Eastern Steamship suffered the first loss of one of its steamers as a result of an accident. At about 3:30 in the morning of September 23, *Bay State* was feeling her way toward Portland harbor through fog when she went hard aground on Holycomb Ledge off Cape Elizabeth. Although her Captain, Levi Foran, knew every inch of his route, even when running blind in a fog, it seems that the Portland lightship had been taken from its usual station for repairs and replaced by a whistling buoy. Unfortunately, *Bay State*'s pilot, unaccustomed to this change, mistook a similar buoy for this one and changed course accordingly. As a result *Bay State* ran up on the ledge a few seconds later.

During the following day all of the passengers and crew and most of the cargo were removed safely, and the company made arrangements to have its stranded steamer salvaged. But in the stormy weather that ensued *Bay State*, trapped as she was on the ledge, was blown apart before the salvage company could start its work. Since the crest of summer travel had passed by September, *Ransom B. Fuller* was left to cover the route alone, making sailings from each port only three nights a week for the rest of the season.

The following April, about the time the season of 1917 was getting started, the United States, after having carefully avoided armed participation in the European conflict for nearly three years, was finally obliged, by the blatant sinking of its neutral ships in the Atlantic, to declare war on the German Empire. As was to be the case again in 1941, however, the United States found itself without an adequate Navy or merchant marine at a time when it was at war with powerful nations on the other side of the Atlantic Ocean. As a result, the government made it known that it was prepared to pay top dollar for any merchant vessels that could be made available.

Calvin Austin and his associate directors were faced with a dilemma. If Eastern sold several of its steamers to the government at the attractive prices being offered, the company could substantially reduce

Bay State ashore near Cape Elizabeth, September, 1916.
(Marine Museum at Fall River, Massachusetts)

City of Bangor as rebuilt after a fire while at dock in 1913. Note larger walking-beam housing.

Massachusetts (left background) departing from Boston in the evening for New York, and *Belfast* (right foreground) departing from Boston in the evening for Bangor, about 1912.

City of Rockland at her wharf in Boston.
(R. Loren Graham Collection, Steamship Historical Society, University of Baltimore Library)

its burdensome debt, perhaps even remove it alto-gether. On the other hand, by selling its steamers, in particular the newer and larger steel-hulled steamers which would be of interest to the government, the company would have to reduce significantly its rev-enue-producing services.

Eastern's ultimate decision was to take advan-tage of the opportunity and sell a large number of its most valuable steamers at the end of the 1917 season. There was some advantage, in any event, to selling the three large steamers Eastern had inherited from the New Haven Railroad, for with the opening of the Cape Cod Canal these vessels designed for speed had become unnecessarily expensive to operate. In the sale to the government the two large Boston steamers, *Massachusetts* and *Bunker Hill,* brought $1,350,000 each. The government also paid $1,150,000 for *Old Colony,* and $380,000 apiece for the four former Met-ropolitan Line freight steamers. *Prince George* and *Prince Arthur,* as noted, had been requisitioned by the British, but now Eastern also sold *Boston,* the Yarmouth

route's spare steamer, for $110,000. Although fitted with guns and renamed U.S.S. *Cambridge,* this vessel was never actually used by the Navy and was finally scrapped in 1926.

In the Navy, *Massachusetts,* renamed *Shawmut,* and *Bunker Hill,* renamed *Aroostook* were converted to minelayers, and assigned to the North Sea Squadron. Both were so thoroughly rebuilt for their military service that there was never any possi-bility of their return to the passenger trade after the war. Both therefore remained in the Navy, although the name of the former *Massachusetts* was later changed from *Shawmut* to *Oglala,* and both appar-ently served for a time as aircraft tenders after the war. There are several contradictory accounts of the fate of *Old Colony,* but the most reliable seems to be that she was sold to the French government and tor-pedoed in the Bay of Biscay in 1918.

As long as they were unloading tonnage so freely, Eastern also sold its unsatisfactory Kennebec River sternwheeler, *City of Augusta* in 1917. Since

Belfast backing into her wharf at Boston.
(R. Loren Graham Collection, Steamship Historical Society, University of Baltimore Library)

Belfast (Marine Museum at Fall River, Massachusetts)

busses meeting the steamers at Bath could now transport passengers far more quickly to upriver destinations, Eastern had stopped running its transfer steamer at the end of the 1915 season, and *City of Augusta*, had been in lay-up for two years waiting for a buyer. *City of Augusta* was sold first to the Merrill-Stevens shipyard in Jacksonville, Florida, where, renamed *St. Johns*, she was employed ferrying workers to their wartime shipyard in South Jacksonville. After the war, she became a nightclub near Savannah for a short time, but in the early 1920s she was destroyed in a fire.

In the fall of 1917 the government also chartered all three steamers of the International Line, *Calvin Austin*, *Governor Dingley*, and *Governor Cobb*, for use as training ships, and *Ransom B. Fuller* for use as a barracks ship in New London, Connecticut. With so many of the vessels in its fleet either sold or requisitioned for war service, the most suitable steamers available for the Boston-New York route (still called the "Metropolitan Line") were *Belfast* and *Camden*

from the Bangor Line with just 200 staterooms each and very limited cargo space. Although *Belfast* and *Camden* were fairly fast and had managed as much as eighteen or nineteen knots on favorable occasions, they were not fast enough to maintain the schedule on the New York-to-Boston run established by *Massachusetts* and *Bunker Hill*. Consequently, in 1918 the departure time from both New York and Boston had to be moved up one full hour to 5:00 P.M. To replace *Belfast* and *Camden* on the Bangor route, *City of Rockland* and *City of Bangor* were taken from the Kennebec run and returned to the Bangor Line. Thus through the season of 1918 Eastern could offer no service at all on the International Line, the Kennebec Line, or the Boston-Portland Line; and service only with smaller steamers on the Bangor Line and the company's primary route, the New York-to-Boston Metropolitan Line.

Shortly after she had been requisitioned by the government, *Calvin Austin* was called upon for an unusual errand of mercy. On December 6, 1917,

Governor Dingley at her wharf in Boston.
(R. Loren Graham Collection, Steamship Historical Society, University of Baltimore Library)

as a result of confused whistle signals, a Norwegian grain carrier entering the harbor at Halifax rammed into the munitions ship *Mont Blanc*. The result was an explosion that rocked the entire city and left hundreds dead and many seriously injured. As soon as news of this disaster reached Boston, *Calvin Austin*, with doctors, nurses, food, and as many supplies as she could carry, was dispatched to the scene. Although *Calvin Austin* herself nearly foundered in a storm she encountered on the way, she was the first rescue ship to arrive at Halifax after the explosion.

As it happened, *Old Colony*, then in government service, was in Halifax harbor at the time of the explosion, but as she was docked about seven miles away from *Mont Blanc*, she was not damaged in the explosion. During the emergency, therefore, *Old Colony* served for several weeks as a temporary hospital ship.

At last free of debt and staggering interest payments, if indeed also rather short of steamers, Eastern Steamship underwent yet another corporate reorganization in the late fall of 1917, shortly after many of its ships had been sold or chartered to the government. The new name of the company, of which Calvin Austin was again President, Josiah Hayden, Chairman of the Board, and Galen Stone, Treasurer (and now also Vice-President) was Eastern Steamship Lines, Incorporated, under which it was to operate for another thirty-eight years.

The war ended in November, 1918, and by the time the 1919 season was to begin enough of Eastern's steamers had been returned and, when necessary, cleaned up and refurbished, to return to more normal services of sorts. The company's larger steamers which had been sold outright to the government, of course, were never to return, so for the next several years, until new steamers appropriate for the route could be ordered, Eastern Steamship had to manage as well as it could by operating smaller steamers on the lucrative New York-to-Boston route.

For the season of 1919 *Calvin Austin*, with her much larger passenger capacity, was placed on the New York-Boston route with *Belfast*, in place of *Camden*, leaving only *Governor Dingley* and *Governor Cobb* to cover the International route between Boston and St. John. *Belfast*, however, met with a freak accident on her first trip of the season. On the morning of April 16, she was coursing through the Cape Cod Canal on her way to Boston shortly before dawn when, just as the Sagamore Bridge had opened to let

her pass through, *Belfast* was caught in a cross-current so strong that her Quartermaster lost control and the steamer headed straight into the stationary span to the left of the drawbridge. The pilot house and several staterooms forward were completely demolished as *Belfast* slid under the span. The Pilot and Quartermaster, after watching in horror as the solid steel span kept moving inexorably toward them, escaped only by jumping free just seconds before the pilot house was crumpled into splinters under it. Some of the passengers in nearby staterooms were injured but none seriously. After the accident *Camden* had to be brought back on the Metropolitan Line for several trips until *Belfast* could be repaired.

In 1919, once *Belfast* was back on the Boston-New York run, *Camden* returned to the Bangor line to run opposite *City of Bangor*, while *City of Rockland* was assigned to re-establish service on alternate nights between Boston and the Kennebec River ports. That season *Ransom B. Fuller* also offered service only three nights a week in each direction between Boston and Portland.

As *Prince George* and *Prince Arthur* were not returned to the company until the season of 1920, *North Star* of the New York-Portland line continued alone on the Boston-Yarmouth route. During the morning of August 8, 1919, when *North Star* was steaming very cautiously toward Yarmouth harbor through a fog (and one might note that on this coast there are frequent impenetrable fogs through which one cannot pick out even a flashing light more than twenty yards distant), she ran up on underwater rocks with such force that she cracked her hull. During that day, all passengers and crew were taken safely ashore, but *North Star*, still a relatively new ship, had to be abandoned. *Governor Cobb* was assigned to the Yarmouth route to replace *North Star* for the remainder of that season.

Of the ships available to the company in 1920, the two with the largest passenger capacities were *Calvin Austin* and *North Land*. For the next four seasons, from 1920 to 1923, therefore, these two steamers were to cover the summer service between New York and Boston. That year *Governor Cobb*, whose coal-hungry turbines had been a problem for Eastern, was sold to the Peninsular and Occidental Steamship Company of Florida, the line to which she had been regularly chartered during the winters before the war. Now, with Florida's sudden spurt in popularity and Havana becoming an attractive city for tour-

U. S. Navy Minelayer, *Aroostook*, formerly *Bunker Hill* of Eastern Steamship's New York-to-Boston service.

ists (probably in part as a result of the recent introduction of Prohibition in the United States), *Governor Cobb* sailed south in 1920 to run on an all-year schedule between Key West and Havana rather than only in winter.

The British had returned *Prince George* and *Prince Arthur* by 1920, so that this season these smart sisterships were again providing four round trips per week between Boston and Yarmouth. But with *Governor Cobb* sold south and *Calvin Austin* on the New York route, *Governor Dingley* was left to serve the International Line alone for several seasons. With *Belfast* and *Camden* both back on the Boston-Bangor route in 1920, *City of Bangor* was assigned to run oppsite *Ransom B. Fuller* to re-establish daily service between Boston and Portland

As *City of Bangor* was now running to Portland, *City of Rockland* was therefore still alone on the Kennebec route offering sailings from each end only on alternate evenings. With competition from automobiles and trucks seriously eroding the revenues on the Kennebec route, Eastern Steamship concluded that this line was no longer profitable and announced that 1920 would be its last season. Citizens of Bath, Gardiner, and other cities along the Kennebec, convinced that the summer steamer connection to Boston was essential to the local economy, sent a delegation to the officials of Eastern Steamship to ask the company to reconsider. When their pleas failed to

move Eastern's executives to reinstate the service, a group of local citizens formed their own Kennebec Navigation Company and for the seasons of 1921 and 1922 chartered *City of Rockland* from Eastern for the route.

At the end of the 1922 season, however, the independent Kennebec Navigation Company had to admit that it lacked the experience or the facilities, not to mention the capital, to manage *City of Rockland*'s operation profitably. This time Eastern relented and for the season of 1923 again operated *City of Rockland* itself to the Kennebec. But this season ended in tragedy for the handsome *City of Rockland*. For the third time in only seven years one of Eastern's steamers ended its career by running aground as a result of fog. Unlike *Bay State* in 1916 or *North Star* in 1919, however, *City of Rockland*'s grounding came when she was leaving port in the evening rather than entering it in the early morning. On September 23, near the end of the season, *City of Rockland* pulled away from her wharf in Bath on schedule at 6:00 P.M., in spite of a thick fog on the river, and headed cautiously down the Kennebec toward the Atlantic. At 7:30 P.M., as she was approaching the mouth of the river navigating carefully through the surrounding gray mist with nothing to guide her pilots but the distant moan of a fog horn or the solemn pealing of a buoy, *City of Rockland* ran hard aground on Dix Island. As with the two earlier acci-

Harvard (temporarily renamed *Charles*) as a troop transport in the English Channel during the First World War. (Marine Museum at Fall River, Massachusetts)

dents to the line's steamers, all of the passengers and crew were removed safely, but *City of Rockland* had cracked her keel, and the line, by then committed in any event to retiring its wooden-hulled sidewheelers, elected not to have her repaired. Once hauled off and patched, *City of Rockland* was towed to East Boston and laid up, but then a year later dismantled. What remained was later towed out to the appropriately named Little Misery Island and set afire.

By this time Eastern Steamship had decided that one steamer, *Ransom B. Fuller*, running on alternate evenings from each port, would suffice for the declining traffic on the Boston-Portland run. One might want to remember that only fourteen years before both *Ransom B. Fuller* and *Bay State* had been considerably rebuilt, in the process giving *Ransom B. Fuller* more staterooms than any other vessel operated by the company, in order to accommodate the heavy traffic demands of the Portland route. With *City of Bangor* now superfluous, Eastern assigned her to the unprofitable Kennebec line to replace her former running mate. She did not last long on this line, however, for Eastern finally gave up the Kennebec route altogether at the end of the 1925 season.

For the Eastern Steamship Company, as for the country in general, the post-war world of the early 1920s was emerging as very different from the world before the war. For Eastern, as well as for all short-haul steamer lines, the particular change that had to be dealt with was the rapidly increasing popularity of automobiles and trucks. As recently as the two decades before the war, when travel was becoming fashionable in America, short-haul lines operating large wooden-hulled steamers such as those on some of Eastern Steamship's routes, could hardly keep up with the burgeoning traffic demands. After the war, however, many of those people who could afford to travel preferred to do so in their own automobiles. Many who did choose to make part of a trip by steamer wanted to take their automobile aboard with them, but the pre-war steamers operated by Eastern Steamship were not equipped to handle more than a few automobiles on their freight decks. Also, shippers who had found transportation of goods by sea both convenient and inexpensive in the pre-war years now discovered that gasoline-powered trucks could pick up goods right at their doors and deliver them directly to their destinations. Another problem for the steamer

67

Calvin Austin, which served on Eastern's Boston-New York route 1919-1923 after the company's larger steamers had been sold for war service. (Marine Museum at Fall River, Massachusetts)

North Land, which usually operated on Eastern's New York-Portland service, ran opposite *Calvin Austin* on the Boston-New York route after the larger steamers had been sold for war service. (Marine Museum at Fall River, Massachusetts)

lines was that operating costs—coal, oil, maintenance, dockage, and especially labor—were rising in the 1920s far faster than it was possible to raise the rates for passengers or cargo at a time when business was already on the decline.

Other national movements in the 1920s were also affecting the short-haul steamer lines of New England. Washington, Oregon, and Montana were replacing Maine as the primary suppliers of pine lumber, even to East Coast areas. The myriad small family-owned fish canneries of northern Maine were losing business to larger canning factories in other parts of the country. A particularly serious loss was the move of most fabric manufacturers from eastern Massachusetts to the South, nearer the source of raw cotton, where both land and labor were less expensive.

Neither the short-haul marine services nor the comfortable wooden-hulled sidewheelers that served on them were to disappear abruptly in the 1920s, of course. Some were to be around for many years more.

But the demand for this type of transportation was clearly beginning a precipitous decline. Many overnight steamer lines in America continued to operate large superannuated steamers on routes providing ever-decreasing revenues until they simply went out of business. Calvin Austin, and other executives of the Eastern Steamship Lines, however, were apparently able to perceive that their short-haul overnight routes between Boston and ports along the Maine Coast, the lines that had been the very heart of the company when Charles W. Morse created it—in particular the Boston-Portland and Boston-Kennebec routes, with their largely seasonal traffic and with destinations which could be reached in a matter of a few hours by automobiles or trucks—were not likely to be even minimally profitable much longer. These men were prepared, therefore, to give up these unprofitable lines when the time came that they should and to begin seeking new routes and building a new fleet better adapted to the transportation needs of these rapidly changing times.

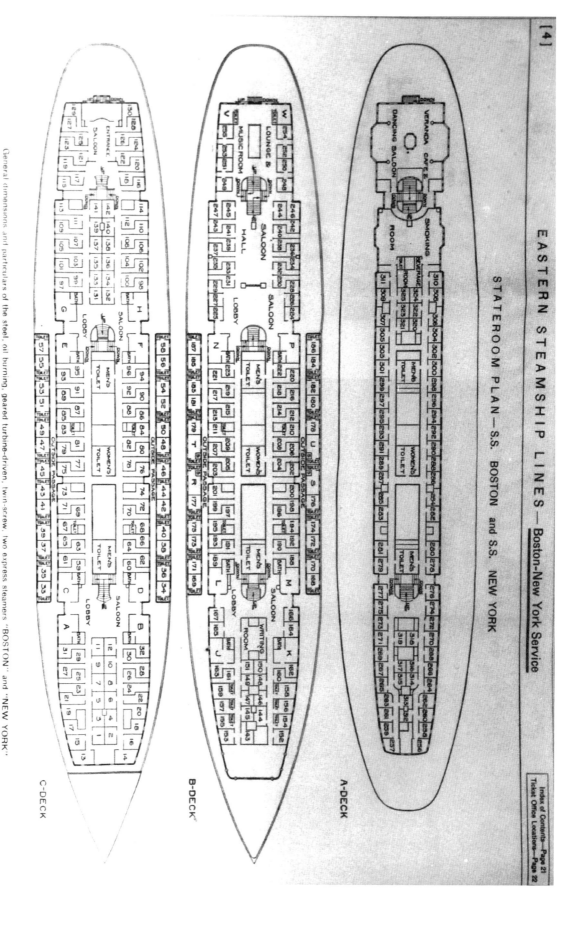

A-DECK

B-DECK

C-DECK

General dimensions and particulars of the steel, oil burning, geared turbine-driven, twin-screw, two express steamers "BOSTON" and "NEW YORK".

Length overall . . . . 402 ft.
Beam, moulded . . . 72 ft. 6 in.

Gross tonnage 5,000
Sleeping space is provided for 800 passengers

Boston and *New York*, stateroom plans.

70

V. New Ships, New Routes, New Directions: 1923-1929

Although Eastern Steamship Lines found itself short of ships in the early 1920s, for the first time in its history, after the profitable sales of many vessels and the charters of others during the war, the company was not short of capital. By 1923, Eastern was prepared to embark in bold new directions: adding a fleet of small cargo vessels; establishing new routes that were less seasonal or warm-water winter routes for vessels otherwise employed only on summer routes in New England or Canada; and building new modern ships adapted changing travel and cargo demands and to a variety of services.

One of Eastern's first moves after the war was to build or to purchase several small sea-going cargo vessels. In the past Eastern had either continued to run its passenger vessels on a curtailed schedule, mainly to carry cargo, or cancelled service altogether during the winter months when passenger traffic was light. But these passenger vessels were often both unnecessarily expensive to operate and ill-adapted to the rigors of winter weather on the Maine Coast. In the 1920s, if the line were to cancel or even curtail its services during the winter months, it faced the danger of losing cargo contracts to the trucking companies which could operate throughout the year. Eastern's solution, therefore, was to place small ocean-going freighters on its Maine Coast lines during the winter.

In 1920 the 250-foot *Norfolk* was built for the company. The similar *Lake Falun*, built in 1919, and *Lake Floravista* and *Lake Feodora*, both built in 1920, became *Sandwich*, *Falmouth*, and *Sagamore* when puchased by Eastern in 1923. That same year the somewhat smaller *Wilton* and *Cornish* were built for Eastern at Sparrow's Point, Maryland. With these vessels, which were admittedly slow but therefore also inexpensive to operate, Eastern could maintain an all-year freight service on routes which provided passenger service only seasonally without losing shipping contracts to trucks.

Eastern's first major step toward diversification was its purchase of the Old Dominion Line on December 31, 1923, although the actual incorporation of the Old Dominion Line into the Eastern Steamship Lines was not concluded until 1925. The Old Dominion Line had since its founding in 1867 operated ocean-going passenger and cargo steamships between New York and Norfolk and between New York and Richmond. About 1900 the New York-Richmond route was given up. Instead the line built two small steamers, *Berkeley* and *Brandon*, to provide a daily overnight service between Norfolk and Richmond. Passengers and cargo bound for Richmond transferred to one of these steamers at Norfolk.

For much of its history the Old Dominion Line also operated a fleet of small sidewheel steamboats to the many rivers and inlets within a day's run from Norfolk. These steamers touched at the plantations or towns in the area and brought their produce, usually cotton or vegetables, to the Old Dominion dock in Norfolk to be transferred to the New York boat. In the early 1920s, however, trucks had taken over most of these routes and the Old Dominion Line no longer operated its connecting steamers.

In the years shortly before the First World War, the Old Dominion Line's daily sailings from both New York and Norfolk were maintained by three steamers: the sistership *Hamilton* and *Jefferson* built in 1899, both 305.8 feet in length when built, but later lengthened to 351.8 feet, and the similar *Madison*, built in 1911. Also in occasional service was the 300-foot *Jamestown* of 1894. Every day one steamer left New York at noon to arrive in Norfolk at 7:30 the following morning, and a steamer sailed from Norfolk at 7:30 each evening to arrive in New York the following afternoon at 3:00 P.M.

Like other coastal steamer lines, the Old Dominion had suffered serious revenue losses when the government took its ships for service in the First World War. After the war the company also encountered problems similar to those that other steamship companies were facing in this era, mainly shifting markets and escalating costs of labor and maintenance. As a consequence, in April, 1920, the venerable Old Dominion Line, without actually going out of business, simply stopped running its steamships. A group

Boston upbound in East River, New York.
(Harry Cotterell, Jr. Collection, Steamship Historical Society, University of Baltimore Library)

of Norfolk businessmen, however, who depended on the Old Dominion Line, organized a new company called the Old Dominion Transportation Company in June, 1920. This new company then chartered the steamers *Hamilton* and *Jefferson* from the former Old Dominion Steamship Company and revived the Norfolk-New York sailings, though on a curtailed and somewhat irregular schedule.[1]

Early in 1923 the Eastern Steamship Lines, then actively seeking new markets and new routes, particularly all-year routes, purchased both the Old Dominion Steamship Company and the Old Dominion Navigation Company and took over the operation of the New York-Norfolk route. With its purchase of the original Old Dominion Steamship Company, Eastern also acquired its four steamships, *Madison*, *Jefferson*, *Hamilton*, and *Jamestown*, with which Eastern restored regularly-scheduled daily service from each port.

In its program of renewing its fleet with modern vessels which could be adapted to serve on a variety of routes, Eastern Steamship was able to take advantage of new government programs set forth in the Merchant Marine Acts of 1920 and 1928. During the war years, 1917 and 1918, the government of the United States was embarrassed to realize the weakness of the American merchant marine and the lack of privately operated American merchant ships that could be made available in this time of national emergency. After the war the Congress on the one hand wanted to use federal authority to encourage the construction of modern and well-equipped privately-owned American vessels which could become available in a time of national emergency. On the other hand, although American shipping had to compete with the lines of other countries which subsidized shipbuilding, in the United States Democrat and Republican politicians alike were adamantly opposed to granting government subsidies to private businesses.

The Merchant Marine Act of 1920 was a compromise. In its preamble it stated its objectives as follows:

> That it is necessary for the national defense and for the proper growth of its foreign and domestic commerce that the United States shall have a merchant marine of the best-equipped and most suitable types of vessels sufficient to carry the greater proportion of its commerce and serve as a naval or military auxiliary in time of war or national emergency ultimately to be owned and operated privately by citizens of the United States.[2]

This act set aside $125,000,000 of federal funds from which the United States Shipping Board (established during the war emergency, but now continued during peacetime) could offer long-term loans at low interest for the construction in American ship-

Hamilton of the Old Dominion Line. *Hamilton*, her sistership, *Jefferson*, and the similar *Madison* were the steamers of the Old Dominion Line when Eastern Steamship purchased this company in 1923. (Marine Museum at Fall River, Massachusetts)

yards of American-flag ships "of the best and most efficient type...provided such vessels shall be fitted and equipped with the most modern and most efficient and economical engines and machinery."

The most pressing need of the Eastern Steamship Company in the 1920s was for larger steamers on the New York-to-Boston route, and it was for the construction of these steamers that Eastern first took advantage of the long-term low-interest loans available from the Shipping Board. Steamers for Eastern's summer service between New York and Boston, however, had rather specific and unique requirements. Their hulls had to be narrow enough to navigate safely through the Cape Cod Canal but seaworthy enough to remain stable in the often heavy seas through Block Island Sound. And, even with fairly narrow hulls, these ships needed sufficiently large passenger and cargo capacity, preferably more than any of the earlier steamers operated on this route, to render this seasonal operation profitable. The superstructures on the two earlier pairs of passenger steamers on this line, *Yale* and *Harvard* or *Massachusetts* and *Bunker Hill*, which had to sail through the rougher waters off the Cape but were not designed to pass through the

canal, had not been significantly wider than their hulls, which had somewhat limited their capacity. Now that the less treacherous route through the Cape Cod Canal was available, it was possible to design the new steamers for this route with relatively narrow hulls and with much wider superstructures built over cantilevered guards like the steamers on the other Long Island Sound overnight lines.

In 1923 Eastern asked Theodore Ferris, at the time one of the country's leading naval architects for commercial vessels, to prepare designs for the proposed new Boston boats, and awarded the Maryland Steel Company at Sparrow's Point (near Baltimore) the contract to build them. The new steamers, named *Boston* and *New York*, were completed in time for the 1924 season at a cost of $1,750,000 apiece, of which $912,500 for each steamer was financed with long-term, low-interest loans from the Shipping Board. With an overall length of 402 feet and an extreme beam of 72.5 feet (over a hull with a beam of 50 feet), *Boston* and *New York* were larger than any of the previous steamers on the route. Each carried 345 staterooms, almost as many as the Fall River Line's larger *Priscilla*.

Boston upbound in East River, New York, passing under Triboro Bridge.
(Photo by William King Covell from the Collection of William H. Ewen, Jr.)

New York eastbound in Long Island Sound from the deck of one of the Fall River Line steamers.
(Harry Cotterell Collection, Steamship Historical Society, University of Baltimore Library)

Boston was the first to come from the builders. She made her first sailing from Boston on June 4, replacing *North Land* and running opposite *Calvin Austin* until *New York* arrived to make her maiden trip on the Fourth of July.

No one ever called *Boston* or *New York* beautiful. They certainly did not evoke the graceful lines of *Yale* and *Harvard*. Roger Williams MacAdam, author of several fascinating books about Long Island Sound steamboats, when he first sighted *Boston* rounding the Battery and heading up the North River on her maiden arrival in New York, commented: "I thought Ferris could design ships!" Frank M. Dunbaugh, Jr., Vice-President of the rival Colonial Line (New York to Providence), was probably closer to the truth than he intended when he quipped that Eastern's only stipulation when asking Ferris to design *Boston* and *New York* had been that they "accommodate as many people as possible on hulls that can pass through the Cape Cod Canal."

Although their overhanging guards classified them as Sound-type steamers, in order to maximize their capacity Ferris incorporated many aspects in the design of *Boston* and *New York* more common to ocean-going ships. For example, Ferris abandoned the long tradition on Long Island Sound and Maine Coast steamers of locating staterooms along both sides of the Saloon Deck and the Gallery Deck, and leaving an impressive lounge area (often two decks high) between the stateroom rows aft of the engine housing. Instead, on *Boston* and *New York*, as on most ocean-going steamers, staterooms, separated only by narrow corridors, and a majority of them "inside staterooms" (that is, windowless), filled virtually all available space on two decks. A third passenger deck also consisted of staterooms separated only by corridors, though at the after end were two attractive and comfortable public rooms. In one of them, designed for dancing, an orchestra played modern tunes as the steamer coursed her way up the Sound. The other room was called a "Smoking Room," though it would probably have been designated as a "Bar" had Prohibition not gone into effect a few years earlier. On still another deck above Ferris provided the steamers' navigating officers with a bridge spanning the full beam of the vessel rather than a pilot house which was more typical on overnight boats.

Interestingly, the terms "Saloon Deck" and "Gallery Deck" in general use for decades on the steamers of Long Island Sound or the Maine Coast

did not appear on *Boston* or *New York*. As on ocean vessels of the era, their passenger decks were listed as "A," "B," "C," and "D."

In many respects *Boston* and *New York* provided passengers with ammenities not available aboard any of their predecessors on the route or even on the great Fall River Line steamers famous for their elegant accommodations. By the 1920s there were many passengers, particularly those travelling with families, who could no longer be content crammed into a tiny cabin furnished only with narrow double-decker bunks, without running water, and located long corridors away from the nearest toilet. The majority of staterooms on *Boston* and *New York* were still of this type (though all of them had sinks with hot and cold running water), since for a short overnight trip businessmen travelling alone often preferred them for their low cost. But for other travellers these steamers also provided twenty larger rooms with comfortable twin beds and with a connecting private bathroom, and over sixty smaller staterooms with adjoining private toilets.

Boston and *New York* were not as fast as any of the earlier steamers on the route, particularly *Yale* and *Harvard*, but now that the route via the Cape Cod Canal was available, they did not need to be. With their twin-screw geared-turbine engines producing 7600 Horsepower, *Boston* or *New York* could work up to a top speed of about nineteen knots when necessary, but with a cruising speed closer to seventeen knots they could cover the route in the required fifteen hours their schedule called for without the enormous oil consumption of the earlier steamers. Fifteen hours allowed a half hour more time than had been scheduled for *Bunker Hill* and *Massachusetts* after they began using the Cape Cod Canal in 1916, for *Boston* and *New York* left each port at 5:30 P.M. and docked at the other end at 8:00 A.M. The saving in fuel easily compensated for the negligible loss of time.

Whether or not they were very speedy and whether or not the marine world's critics considered them as comely as *Yale* or *Harvard*, *Boston* and *New York* proved unwaveringly popular, and even though their service was seasonal, their enormous capacities for both passengers and cargo earned good profits for Eastern Steamship.

Between 1918 and 1924, when Eastern had been operating only smaller steamers on its New York-to-Boston route, the rival Fall River Line had again enjoyed having the bulk of the New York-Boston traf-

New York upbound in East River, New York.

fic to itself. In fact, during these years the Fall River Line had been able to operate two large sidewheelers from each port every night during the busier summer months. But when Eastern placed the new *Boston* and *New York* on the route in 1924, the New England Steamship's Fall River Line again found itself facing a competitor of relatively equal status. And this time the New Haven Railroad, New England Steamship's parent company, was constrained by federal regulations from interfering with the operation of Eastern's Boston line.

    Boston and *New York* were not quite so large as the Fall River Line's summer steamers, the sidewheelers *Commonwealth* of 1908 and *Priscilla* of 1894. But they were comparable. To be sure, both the decor and the service on the Fall River steamers represented the essence of elegance. On the other hand, by the 1920s the Victorian or Edwardian grandeur of the Fall River steamers was beginning to be viewed as old fashioned, even dowdy. The Boston boats were not so elegant as the Fall River Line's steamers, but they were new, and in their very simplicity of style they better reflected the tastes of this post-war era. In this age of the Charleston, these new Boston boats pro-

vided a dance hall where a band played lively modern tunes until midnight. In the carpeted saloons of the Fall River Line steamers, on the other hand, a sedate ensemble played what some might call "tea-time music" until about nine in the evening.

    The single strongest draw in the popularity of *Boston* and *New York* over the Fall River Line's steamers was that they could deliver their passengers right in downtown Boston in time for a full day of business. However elegant or graceful a voyage aboard one of the grand Fall River sidewheelers might have been, a passenger who wanted to be in Boston in time to start the usual working day had to be awake, dressed, and ready to disembark when the steamer docked in Fall River at 5:30 in the morning. It is not surprising that even many of the Fall River Line's most devoted patrons often chose the line only for the return voyage, while for the trip up to Boston they preferred to travel by Eastern Steamship.

    Barely two months into the first season with their new steamers Eastern came close to losing *Boston*. On her way to New York on the evening of July 21, 1924, *Boston* emerged from the Cape Cod Canal into Buzzard's Bay about 11:00 P.M. and found her-

Boston beached at Newport, Rhode Island, shortly after she had been rammed by the freighter *Swift Arrow* in July, 1924. (Marine Museum at Fall River, Massachusetts)

self steaming into a thick blinding fog. About midnight, shortly after she had passed Newport, the officers on the bridge were alerted by the ominous sound of a steamer's whistle obviously not very far away. As a precaution the pilot ordered *Boston*'s engines stopped and then into full reverse, but the order came too late. As her officers peered anxiously into the gray nothingness that surrounded them, waiting for some further hint of the other steamer's location, the sharp black prow of the freighter *Swift Arrow* suddenly came crashing into *Boston*'s port side about amidships. With an enormous gash in her side, *Boston* immediately began taking water and started slipping slowly under.

Captain Alfred Call, as soon as he became aware that his ship was sinking, ordered all passengers into lifeboats and told his radioman to send out the S.O.S. signal.

At that time the Fall River Line, as yet unaffected by the degree to which *Boston* and *New York* would drain off its passenger traffic, was still operating two large steamers in each direction every night during the summer. Headed toward New York that night were both *Priscilla* and *Providence*. As these steamers were due at their Manhattan piers at 7:00

A.M., an hour before *Boston*, they were then already several miles ahead of her. Since they were also at the place where they passed the eastbound boats—*Commonwealth* and *Plymouth* that night—all four Fall River steamers were at about the same position, near Race Point off New London, and would require about an hour to reach the sinking *Boston*.

Even though the Fall River Line was Eastern's most competitive rival, the rules of the sea as always took precedence, and all four of these big sidewheelers picked up to full speed, even in the fog, to reach *Boston* as soon as possible. *Priscilla*, the first to arrive, slowed as she approached the scene to avoid plowing into any of *Boston*'s lifeboats. Since *Boston* had lost steam, *Priscilla* also began blowing her whistle to serve as a guide to other steamers searching for *Boston* in the fog.

Most of *Boston*'s passengers, save four who had been killed in the crash, were taken aboard *Priscilla* or one of the other Fall River steamers. Once the rescue operations had been completed, Captain Edward Geer of*Commonwealth*, aware that *Boston* would probably soon go under and would certainly be lost before any rescue vessels could be brought to

George Washington of the Old Dominion Line. *George Washington* and her sistership, *Robert E. Lee*, were added to the Old Dominion service by Eastern Steamship in 1924 and 1925.

the scene, attempted to tow her to safety. But with *Boston* already heeling to port and way down at the bow, she kept veering dangerously off course and dragging the stern of *Commonwealth* with her. At this point Captain Geer made a decision which could easily have become a serious mistake. After he had eased *Commonwealth* (the largest steamer on the Sound!) right alongside the sinking *Boston*, he ordered his crew to lash these two large steamers together. With the sinking *Boston* virtually hanging from the side of his *Commonwealth*, Geer managed to maneuver the two vessels into the safety of Newport harbor. Here *Boston* was safely beached.

Since *Boston* was to be out of service through most of her first season, *Calvin Austin* was brought back on the run until *Boston* returned shortly before the busy Labor Day weekend.

The following season, with these new and larger steamers on the New York-to-Boston route, both *Calvin Austin* and *North Land* became available to improve service on Eastern's other routes. In 1925 *Calvin Austin* revived summer passenger service on the New York-Portland route, which had been served only by cargo steamers since 1917. With Nova Scotia

growing in popularity as a picturesque vacation area, the smaller steamers of the Boston-Yarmouth route had been unable to handle the increased demand for bookings. In 1925 the much larger *North Land* was placed on this route running opposite *Prince George*, while *Prince Arthur* was transferred to the International Line to assist *Governor Dingley*.

Late in 1924 and early in 1925 the two new ships, *George Washington* and *Robert E. Lee*, Eastern had ordered to replace the outdated vessels on its Old Dominion Divison, arrived from the builders. Although *George Washington* was apparently financed privately, Eastern again took advantage of the Merchant Marine Act of 1920 to arrange a low-interest loan of a million dollars from the government for the construction of *Robert E. Lee*. Also designed by Theodore Ferris, *George Washington* and *Robert E. Lee*, with their nicely sheered black hulls, white superstructures, and single black smokestacks, were attractive small ocean liners in appearance. With these trim new steamships on the Norfolk route, *Hamilton* and *Jefferson* of 1899 were placed in layup. But, as the daily sailings for Norfolk during the summer season required three vessels in operation, *Madison* of

1911 remained in service with *George Washington* and *Robert E. Lee*. Old Dominion's older and smaller *Jamestown*, however, was sold for scrap.

Since at the time the Old Dominion Line had yet not been officially incorporated into the Eastern Steamship Lines, when *George Washington* and *Robert E. Lee* first came out they carried the colors of the Old Dominion Line on their stacks. Later in the year, however, they began to carry Eastern Steamship's distinctive houseflag, a dark blue burgee with a single white "E" within it, which Eastern added to the stacks of all of its steamers at about this time.

During the winters of 1924-25, 1925-26 and 1926-27, Eastern's new *George Washington* and *Robert E. Lee* were chartered to the Clyde Line. With southern Florida becoming popular as a winter resort during the early 1920s, the Clyde Line had decided to inaugurate twice-weekly sailings from New York to Jacksonville and Miami during the winter months. Though this line had also asked Theodore Ferris to design two sistership for the route, until these steamers were completed, the line chartered Eastern's Old Dominion steamers. During the winters that *George Washington* and *Robert E. Lee* were running to Mi-

ami, *Hamilton* and *Jefferson* were brought out of lay-up to cover Eastern's New York-Norfolk route with *Madison*.

It seems that 1925 was a busy year for Eastern Steamship, for in this year the company not only added fine new steamships for its Old Dominion service, but it also bought two other smaller steamer lines. One was the Gulf and Southern Steamship Company, which operated two freighters and one small passenger steamer between Tampa and New Orleans. Though it was owned by Eastern after 1925, this line was never actually incorporated into the company. The other, probably purchased to eliminate competition with Eastern's Old Dominion Division, was the Richmond and New York Steamship Company and with it the line's three small cargo steamers (which had been war surplus vessels similar to the freighters named for lakes that Eastern had earlier purchased from the government): *Virginia Dispatch*, *Virginia Express*, and *Virginia Limited*.

Since Old Dominion's James River overnight line from Norfolk to Richmond had not been revived after the company withdrew all of its services in 1920, the two attractive small night boats, *Berkeley* and *Bran-*

George Washington (Marine Museum at Fall River, Massachusetts)

Yarmouth (Marine Museum at Fall River, Massachusetts)

don, each roughly 200 feet in length, had been left without employment. *Berkeley* was sold in 1923 for a service on the Great Lakes where she was renamed *Virginia*. Her sistership, *Brandon*, Eastern brought north for the season of 1925 to inauguarate a new line—or in a sense to revive one long abandoned—making two sailings a week from Portland all the way up the Maine coast to Eastport with a stop at Rockland along the way. This new route did not prove profitable, however, and was dropped at the end of the season.

The year 1925 was also one in which Eastern Steamship, now clearly committed to longer ocean routes less seasonal and less vulnerable to automobile competition, recognized the need to cancel some of its less profitable short-haul lines. As noted earlier, Eastern gave up its faltering Kennebec route at the end of the 1925 season. *City of Bangor*'s arrival in Boston after her overnight run from Bath on the morning of September 9, 1925, marked the end for the line with which Charles W. Morse had started the Eastern Steamship Company a quarter of a century before. That very evening *City of Bangor* was transferred to the Boston-Portland line. With traffic rapidly giving

way to automobiles and trucks on this relatively short route, the company had decided to run this smaller steamer, making three round trips per week, in place of the "enlarged" *Ransom B. Fuller*, most of whose 265 staterooms had lately been remaining empty during her nightly sailings between Boston and Portland.

Ransom B. Fuller was sold only two weeks later to the Boston, New York, and Southern Steamship Company. Lest readers start scratching their heads at the mention of a steamship line they had never heard of, or wonder how anyone could conceive of operating the aging and awkward wooden-hulled sidewheeler *Ransom B. Fuller* between Boston and New York, let alone to anywhere "Southern," one must here hastily add that this was the rather grand sounding name of a small company managed by its single owner, namely Charles L. Dimon. Dimon collected superannuated steamboats like seashells. Although he often announced eleborate plans for each of the dowager steamers he purchased, most of them ended up rotting slowly at his wharves near Newburgh on the Hudson River. Dimon's most successful operation was running the large excursion steamer *Mandalay* between Manhattan and the beaches and resorts at At-

Evangeline at the America's Cup races, Newport, in 1930.
(W. King Covell photograph, Marine Museum at Fall River, Massachusetts)

lantic Highlands in New Jersey and on "Moonlight Cruises" on summer evenings. *Ransom B. Fuller* he bought specifically with the intention of starting a new low-rate overnight line to Albany in competititon with Morse's Hudson River Night Line, and she was even spruced up at the yard of Thomas Marvel in Newburgh and renamed *Broadway* for the purpose. But the line never materialized, and the old steamer's only further service of note was as a Salvation Army home for unemployed sailors at Staten Island about 1930. She was later partially dismantled at Cornwall-on-Hudson where, at last report, some of her hull timbers were still visible.

The 1925 season was also the last for the small steamer *Monhegan*'s run from Portland to Rockland. In 1919 Eastern had cut service on this route to alternate days with *Monhegan* running alone and had sold the smaller *Mineola* to a line operating out of Pawtucket, Rhode Island. After she too had been sold by Eastern in 1925, *Monhegan* spent one season on the route between Boston and Gloucester, but then joined her former running mate on Narragansett Bay, where in the mid-1930s she served mostly on the daily run from Providence to Block Island and return.

Monhegan was badly damaged at her dock in Providence in the 1938 Hurricane, which had been at its most destructive in Narragansett Bay. With her engines removed, *Monhegan* was later towed down to Prudence Island in Narragansett Bay theoretically to be used as a floating night club. But her new owners apparently had trouble floating a loan let alone a night club, and *Monhegan* was simply left there to be gradually claimed by the elements.

For the seasons of 1926 and 1927 Eastern made one final effort both to preserve the Boston-Portland Line and to maintain a profitable steamer service to the nearer Maine Coast formerly served by the Kennebec boats by extending the Portland Line's route during the height of the summer season. The two steamers placed on this route in 1926, the grand old wooden-hulled sidewheeler *City of Bangor* with 170 staterooms and the compact steel-hulled propeller steamer *Brandon* with 46 staterooms, could hardly be considered a matched pair, but they were available. One of these steamers left Boston at 6:00 every evening to arrive in Portland at 4:00 the following morning, not exactly the hour of the day when people vacationing in Maine are eager to meet weekend guests arriving in Portland. At 8:00 A.M. the steamer sailed again for Boothbay Harbor near the mouth of the Kennebec River where she docked at 11:00 A.M. Returning she sailed from Boothbay Harbor at 2:00, from Portland at 7:30, and arrived back in Boston at 5:30 the following morning. This system did not prove particularly popular, however, and lasted only for the two seasons of 1926 and 1927.

The faithful *City of Bangor*, the last sidewheel night boat in Eastern's service, and the last (other than *Governor Dingley*) of Charles W. Morse's original fleet of 1901 in operation on the line, was laid up in East Boston at the end of the 1927 season, never to turn her wheels again. In December, 1933, following a severe snowstorm, *City of Bangor* filled and sank, and was left to rot where she lay.

In 1927, the year *City of Bangor* was retired and just two years after *George Washington* and *Robert E. Lee* had joined the Eastern fleet, the company added another pair of sisterships. *Yarmouth* and *Evangeline*, two exceptionally attractive small ocean liners, also designed by Ferris, were built, as their names suggest, to replace the older steamers on the Boston-Yarmouth run.

Yarmouth and *Evangeline* were constructed at the yard of William Cramp and Sons in Philadelphia. In ordering these two new vessels, Eastern was once again able to arrange financing with long-term loans of $900,000 for each ship though the Shipping Board. At 378 feet in overall length, *Yarmouth* and *Evangeline* were about the same size as *Robert E. Lee* and *George Washington*, though to most observers they were even more attractive. Like the Norfolk boats, they were designed as small ocean liners with black hulls and white superstructures. One notable difference, however, was that *Yarmouth* and *Evangeline* came out with cruiser sterns, whereas *Robert E. Lee* and *George Washington* carried the more traditional counter sterns. Also, given the different demands of their route, on *Yarmouth* and *Evangeline* a greater proportion of space was devoted to passenger use and less to cargo than on *George Washington* or *Robert E. Lee*. Whereas *Boston* and *New York* had incorporated interior layouts more typical of ocean liners than of inland water steamers, while maintaining the wide superstructure and overhanging guards of inland water night boats, *Yarmouth* and *Evangeline* were designed as ocean-going ships with hulls the full beam of the ship and no overhanging guards. Like *Boston* and *New York*, however, their interior layout consisted

of three decks of staterooms separated only by corridors and without public rooms between them. Instead, they had large and comfortable public rooms the full width of the steamer on the two higher decks. They also provided an even greater proportion of large bedrooms with comfortable beds and connecting private baths than any of the earlier steamers of the company.

Although *Yarmouth* and *Evangeline* sported the arrow-straight plumb bows popular in the 1920s, these sisterships were the first American vessels designed with bulbous bows below the waterline.[3]

The reason *Yarmouth* and *Evangeline* were designed as small ocean liners and with more commodious and comfortable passenger quarters—over twice as many staterooms as either *Prince George* or *Prince Arthur* as well as several large and attractive public rooms—than the Yarmouth overnight route might normally demand, was to enable Eastern to utilize these handsome sisterships for cruising services to Bermuda, the Bahamas, or the Caribbean in the winter months when they were not employed on the Boston-Yarmouth route. Since one of Eastern's weaknesses in its early years had been the seasonal nature of most of its operations, producing vessels which could be adapted to other routes, particularly to short-run cruising, was a major objective of the company's expansion program of the mid-1920s.

For the season of 1927, *Yarmouth*, the first of the pair to be completed, went immediately on the Boston-Yarmouth route with *Prince George*, replacing *North Land*, which now returned to the New York-Portland line for which she had been built. *Calvin Austin*, which had been covering the Portland route for two years, now returned to the Boston-St. John run, the route for which she had been built, with *Governor Dingley*. A few weeks after starting service on the line, *Yarmouth*, which was credited with a cruising speed of over eighteen knots, established a new record on the route by completing the run from Boston to Yarmouth in just twelve and a half hours.

Evangeline, as it happened, was the last ship completed by the original Cramp yard before it closed (although a different owner used the yard and the name during the Second World War). When she was delivered later in the season of 1927, Eastern used her to experiment with a new route on which she made two round trips per week between New York and Yarmouth.

During the winter of 1927-28 Eastern was

able to implement its new policy of finding lucrative winter routes for ships built for its seasonal services in New England or Canada. That winter *Evangeline* was chartered to the Clyde Line to augment that company's New York-Miami service, while *Yarmouth* offered a series of inexpensive thirteen-day cruises out of New York to Miami, Havana, Kingston, and Nassau. The price of one of these cruises, which included all meals aboard the vessel, was $135, or roughly ten dollars a day. Similar cruises aboard either *Yarmouth* or *Evangeline* were repeated in succeeding winters, so that these lovely ships, although built primarily to serve on Eastern's summer routes, could continue to produce revenue throughout the year.

By the mid-1920's the United States government announced plans to purchase the Cape Cod Canal from its private owners in order to widen and deepen it and thus allow this heavily travelled canal to become more accessible to larger vessels and less hazardous in fog. With the removal of the high tolls imposed by the private owners, Eastern Steamship could see that it would save about $300,000 annually, and that it would therefore become financially feasible for the first time for the company to operate passenger vessels on the New York-to-Boston route on an all-year basis. It would not have been profitable to operate the large *Boston* and *New York*, which in any event were not suited to sailing in heavy weather, in the winter. Since the Clyde Line's new ships, *Shawnee* and *Iroquois*, had been delivered in 1927, however, Clyde no longer needed to charter *George Washington* and *Robert E. Lee*. These modern small ocean liners, therefore, were available to take over the New York-Boston route from November to April. Meanwhile the older *Hamilton* and *Jefferson* continued to operate on the Norfolk route with *Madison* in the winter months. Why *Yarmouth* and *Evangeline* were not placed on the Boston run in winter is not clear, although the reason was probably that they had considerably smaller cargo capacities than *Robert E. Lee* and *George Washington*, which rendered them both less suited to the Boston route and better suited to cruising.

For the season of 1928, *Evangeline* again maintained the new New York-to-Yarmouth run, while *Yarmouth* and *Prince George* again ran from Boston to Yarmouth. This season, for some reason, *Prince Arthur*, rather than *Calvin Austin*, again joined *Governor Dingley* on the International Division. Difficult though it may be to believe, *Calvin Austin*, with her enormous passenger capacity, was sent to replace the retired *City of Bangor* on the short and poorly patronized Boston-Portland route. This season, on the three days a week that *Calvin Austin* came into Portland, *Brandon* met her there and took transfer passengers on up to Boothbay Harbor. Apparently this arrangement was no more successful than the earlier one, for it lasted only for the season of 1928, after which the Boston-Portland passenger service was given up altogether, although a regular freight service, usually with *Cornish* and *Wilton*, continued on the route until 1941. For the three seasons from 1929 to 1931 *Calvin Austin* rejoined *Governor Dingley* on the International Line.

By 1929, both *Prince Arthur* and *Prince George* had been sent to the scrapyard. *Brandon* was sold in 1929 to the Quebec and St.Lawrence Navigation Company. Renamed *Riviere du Loup* she began a new career on a ferry service across the St.Lawrence River.

As the season of 1929 was drawing to a close, America was stunned by the unexpected stock market crash in October. When over the next several years the United States suffered the most devastating economic depression in its history, many coastal steamship lines, already buffeted by competition from automobiles and trucks, were not able to survive. With its new routes and with the new and modern ships recently added to its fleet, however, Eastern Steamship Lines found itself in a far better position for survival than most other American steamship lines.

1. John L. Lochhead, "Steamships and Steamboats of the Old Dominion Line," Steamboat Bill, #29, March, 1949.
2. American Bureau of Shipping, The American Merchant Marine, 1933, p. 11.
3. Peter Eisele, "Saga of the Surviving Coastal Twins," Steamboat Bill, #128, Winter, 1973, pp. 209-16.

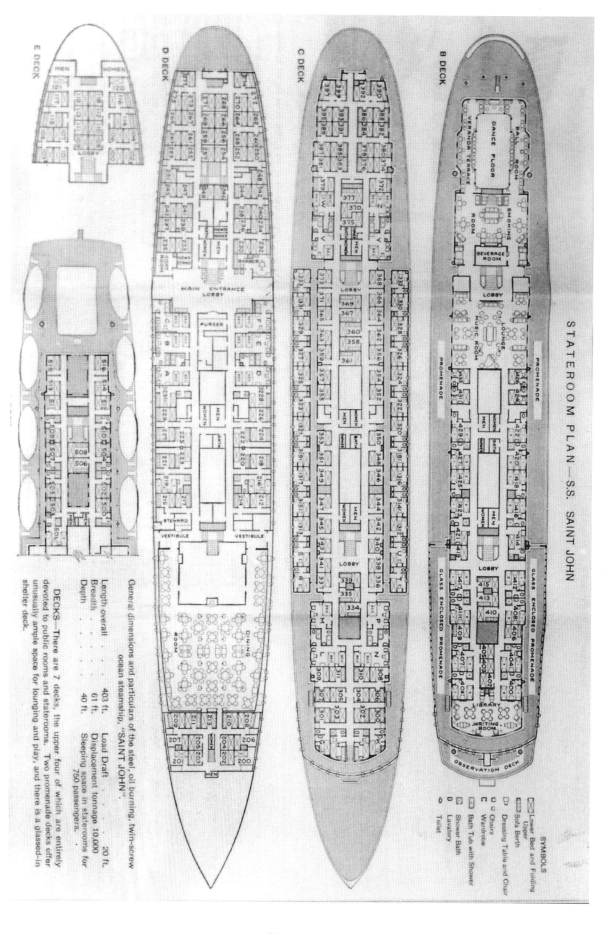

Stateroom plans of *Acadia* and *Saint John.*

STATEROOM PLAN—S.S. SAINT JOHN

SYMBOLS

Lower Bed and Folding Upper
Sofa Berth
Dressing Table and Chair
Chairs
Wardrobe
Bath Tub with Shower
Shower Bath
Lavatory
Toilet

B DECK

C DECK

D DECK

E DECK

General dimensions and particulars of the steel, oil burning, twin-screw ocean steamship, "SAINT JOHN":

Length overall		403 ft.	Load Draft		20 ft.
Breadth		61 ft.	Displacement tonnage 10,000
Depth		40 ft.	Sleeping space in staterooms for 750 passengers.

DECKS—There are 7 decks, the upper four of which are entirely devoted to public rooms and staterooms. Two promenade decks offer unusually ample space for lounging and play, and there is a glassed-in shelter deck.

VI. Eastern Weathers the Depression: 1929-1939

Although the Depression which struck the United States and most of the rest of the Western World as well in 1929 was the final blow for many faltering American coastal steamship companies, Eastern Steamship Lines, as a result of its extraordinary foresight and its recent replacement of most of its fleet with new modern and adaptable vessels, not only survived the Depression but actually enjoyed its greatest prosperity during the 1930's.

As noted earlier, the Boston financial firm of Hayden, Stone and Company had helped Eastern Steamship through the depth of its crisis in the years after the resignation of Charles W. Morse by lending counsel, considerable credit, and even some of its executives. But the stolid Down-Easter, Calvin Austin, as President of the Eastern Steamship Lines, Inc., probably deserves most of the credit for having guided the company from the bleak days of bankruptcy to Eastern's healthy financial state of 1929. In 1930, however, Calvin Austin, who had been Eastern's President since the company was first founded by Charles W. Morse nearly thirty years before, stepped down and was succeeded as President by Captain Eugene E. O'Donnell, former commander of *New York*. One might note the irony that Captain O'Donnell had married into the family of J. Pierpont Morgan, Charles W. Morse's erstwhile nemesis. Captain O'Donnell, unfortunately, died unexpectedly after serving only two years as Eastern's President and was succeeded by Alton B. Sharp.

Apparently Eastern's New York-Boston line was attracting considerable business by 1930 despite the Depression, for that year the company felt the need to charter the brand new steamer *President Warfield* (which was about the same size as *Calvin Austin*, though with considerably less passenger capacity) from the Old Bay Line on the Chesapeake to augment the service of *Boston* and *New York* during the height of the summer season. *President Warfield* was to become better known many years later, first in 1944 when she served as a headquarters ship during the Normandy Invasion, and again in 1947 when, renamed *Exodus*, she was harassed by British destroy-

ers in the Mediterranean while carrying about 2000 Jewish refugees from Europe to Palestine.

By 1930, as a result of the new Merchant Marine Act of 1928, Eastern Steamship was able to order the construction of another pair of sisterships. In 1928 the United States Congress had passed new legislation, which was later signed by President Calvin Coolidge as the Merchant Marine Act of 1928. This act provided even more generous long-term, low-interest loans than the Merchant Marine Act of 1920. By 1928 the American legislators of both parties were still opposed to federal subsidies. The Congress, however, had also become keenly aware that the American merchant marine was seriously suffering from competitition with vessels belonging to nations which did subsidize their merchant ships and which also had less costly guarantees for its seamen or its maintenance crews. The American government in general was very much concerned by statistics showing that an increasing percentage of American international trade was being carried aboard foreign ships. Another factor contributing to the need for new legislation was that in 1927 the United States had joined several other nations in signing the Kellogg-Briand Pact, which placed strict limits on the number of ships participants could maintain in their navies. Although in this era of apparent international peace and cooperation Americans enthusiastically supported this agreement to reduce the number of armed vessels on the oceans, there was nevertheless still some concern that in the event of another emergency the United States might again find itself perilously short of needed tonnage.

The Merchant Marine Act of 1928, therefore, which doubled the amount of federal funds available to the Shipping Board and provided loans with even more generous terms, amended the act of 1920 by specifying that loans would be made for the constructon of vessels "so as to maintain an adequate merchant marine under the United States flag suitable as a naval or military auxiliary in time of need." One provision of this act later to have a particular effect on Eastern Steamship Lines—an effect hardly

President Warfield. This steamer served as an extra boat on Eastern's New York-Boston route in 1930.
Many years later, renamed *Exodus*, she was to carry refugees from Europe to Palestine.
(Viez Collection, Steamship Historical Society, University of Baltimore Library)

anticipated in 1928—was that, until the loans had been repaid, "during any national emergency declared by a proclamation of the President, [vessels constructed with these loans] may be taken or purchased and used by the United States.... In such event the owner shall be paid the fair actual value of the vessel at the time of the taking."[1]

Eastern Steamship lost no time in taking advantage of the favorable terms of the loans offered by the new Merchant Marine Act. As early as 1929 Eastern asked Theodore Ferris to design another pair of sisterships for the company, vessels even larger than *Evangeline* and *Yarmouth*. Late in the season of 1931, therefore, a third pair of attractive small ocean liners, *Acadia* and *Saint John* (and one might note that with this steamship, the "Saint" was never abbreviated), the largest (and last) vessels built for Eastern Steamship Lines, were completed at Newport News Shipbuilding and Drydock Co. With these new vessels, for each of which government loans had provided over $2,000,000, Eastern Steamship Lines had added eight excellent modern steamships, four pair of sisterships, in only seven years.

Acadia and *Saint John* were similar to

Evangeline and *Yarmouth* in general appearance and layout, although at 403 feet in overall length and with one additional passenger deck, considerably larger. They also had more powerful engines and were therefore somewhat faster. Whereas the top speed of *Evangeline* or *Yarmouth* was about eighteen or nineteen knots, both *Acadia* and *Saint John*, in order to comply with the government's requirement that ships constructed under the act of 1928 be of the most modern design and suitable for conversion to military use, had the power to achieve speeds of over twenty-one knots. Like *Evangeline* and *Yarmouth*, *Acadia* and *Saint John* were designed as small ocean liners rather than as typical coastal steamboats, so that they would be able either to serve on Eastern's established seasonal routes in the northeast or to take special off-season cruises to Bermuda, the Bahamas, or the Caribbean. The primary assignment for these new sisterships was to replace *George Washington* and *Robert E. Lee* as the winter boats on the company's overnight line between Boston and New York. During the summers, however, *Acadia* was to take over the New York-to-Yarmouth run, releasing *Evangeline* to join her sistership *Yarmouth* in creating sailings six nights a week between Boston and Yarmouth during the summer season, while *Saint John* was placed on the Boston-St. John route.

Although *Acadia* and *Saint John* had both winter and summer assignments on Eastern's scheduled routes, in the spring and fall, after *Boston* and *New York* had relieved them on the Boston route in April, but before they started their summer routes, and again after their summer routes ended but before they started their winter duty on the Boston run, *Acadia* and *Saint John*, like *Evangeline* and *Yarmouth*, were sent on special short cruises. These were usually one-week cruises from New York or Boston to Bermuda or Nassau. Especially popular were the annual "Easter Cruises" to Bermuda, with *Acadia* sailing from New York and *Saint John* sailing from Boston. As these short cruises were relatively inexpensive, they proved particularly popular during these Depression years and helped Eastern Steamship remain profitable even in this era when many American coastal lines were being forced out of business.

The addition of *Acadia* and *Saint John* to Eastern's fleet and the adaptability of these modern liners to a variety of services meant the end for several of Eastern's older steamers. Although commercial traffic from St. John or Eastport to Boston, mainly shipments of fish, had declined, tourist traffic to these areas was increasing, and tourist travellers often wanted to take their automobiles with them on the ship. Since neither *Calvin Austin* nor *Governor Dingley* had many large comfortable staterooms designed to accommodate travelling families or attractive public rooms for lounging or dancing during the relatively long two-day voyage, and since neither had been built to accommodate automobiles, the new *Saint John* proved far better suited to the changing demands of this route. With this large modern liner alone operating during the summer, and a smaller cargo steamer running through the rest of the year, sufficient to cover the Boston-St. John route, both *Governor Dingley* and *Calvin Austin* were retired at the end of the 1931 season and sold for scrap two years later.

With *Acadia* and *Saint John* serving as the winter boats to Boston, *George Washington* and *Robert E. Lee* could now remain on the New York-Norfolk run all year. *Hamilton* and *Jefferson*, therefore, were also sold for scrap in 1933, although *Madison* remained on the New York-Norfolk route with the newer steamers in order to provide daily sailings. Although it is hard to see how *Acadia* or *Saint John* could fit any other duties into their busy schedules, both somehow found the time to serve briefly each spring as relief steamers on Old Dominion's New York-Norfolk route when the line's three regular steamers went for their annual overhauls.

The year that Eastern added its two finest vessels was also the year that the company retired one of its most beloved older steamers. In the fall of 1931, the popular sidewheeler *J. T. Morse*, although still in excellent condition, was taken off the Rockland-Bar Harbor route at the end of the season and laid up at Camden. From that time Eastern operated one of its smaller propeller steamers, either *Southport* or *Westport*, to Bar Harbor for a few more seasons, but in 1939, by which time there was a bridge and causeway connecting Mt. Desert with the mainland, Eastern gave up the route altogether. In 1933 the Union Navigation Company of New York bought *J. T. Morse*, and this fine sidewheeler, which had for nearly thirty years carried the elite of American society out to their summer palaces on Mt. Desert Island, was renamed *Yankee* and relegated to ferrying crowds of tourists from Battery Park in Manhattan out to the beaches and amusement park at Coney Island.

The season of 1933 was the last for *North Land*, which was sold for scrap the following year. Like many of Eastern's vessels, *North Land* in recent years had been assigned to both a summer route and a winter route. In the summer *North Land* covered the New York-to-Portland route for which she had been built. In the late 1920s and early 1930s, however, she had also been sent south during the winter months to run under charter with the former Eastern Steamship vessel, *Governor Cobb*, on one of Peninsular and Occidental's routes between Florida and Havana. When Peninsula and Occidental brought out its new *Florida* in 1931, however, the line no longer needed to charter *North Land*. In a sense, the addition of *Florida* also brought an end to *North Land*'s New York-Portland service. Although *North Land* in 1933 was still just over twenty years old, like most steamers built for relatively short overnight routes before the First World War, she provided little more than small cabins with double-decker bunks for passengers and only minimal space for automobiles. Since the summer service to Portland was now also attracting tourists as well as commercial travellers, Eastern preferred to charter modern steamers of a type similar to their own *Yarmouth* and *Evangeline* or *Acadia* and *Saint John* for the summer passenger service to

Acadia (Marine Museum at Fall River, Massachusetts)

Portland. For the seasons of 1934 and 1935, therefore, after *North Land* had been retired, Peninsular and Occidental's new *Florida*, a handsome steamer similar to *Yarmouth* and *Evangeline* in size and style, which in that era was employed only in the winter on her run between Miami and Havana, came north in the summer to take over Eastern's New York-Portland route.

The season of 1933 was also the final season for the large Albany night boat, *C. W. Morse*. In 1934, *C. W. Morse* was towed to New Haven and scrapped.

The last of Charles W. Morse's steamers to be removed from Eastern Steamship's roster were *Belfast* and *Camden* of the Boston and Bangor Line. The closing of Eastern's Bangor Line resulted to a large extent from an event that had taken place over two hundred miles from the coast of Maine. In the fall of 1934 the Ward Line steamship, *Morro Castle*, on her way north from Havana, burned in the middle of the night off the coast of New Jersey just hours before she was due to dock in New York. With its tragic cost in human life and with photographs of the burning steamer, not to mention of charred bodies, dominating the pages of virtually every newspaper for several days, the

Morro Castle fire, more than any event since the sinking of *Titanic* twenty-two years before, alerted the American public to the dangers of travel by sea.

As had been the case following the *Titanic* disaster, the investigations into the burning of *Morro Castle* led to a series of new regulations for passenger vessels. Among these was one stating that vessels carrying passengers on routes primarily in the open ocean must have double bottoms and adequate sprinkler systems. *Belfast* and *Camden* did have adequate sprinkler systems, but, as they had been built with only single steel hulls, they could not remain on the route they had served faithfully and safely for over a quarter of a century.

As passenger traffic on the Bangor Line had been declining steadily over the previous decade, Eastern gave no thought to building new ships for this service. The Bangor Line, which had been founded in 1840, nearly a century before, by Menemon Sanford, a pioneer in Maine Coast shipping, was simply given up at the end of the 1935 season after ninety-five years of service. Although the expectation might have been that *Belfast* and *Camden* would follow *Calvin Austin*, *Governor Dingley*, and *North Land* to the scrap yard,

Saint John (Marine Museum at Fall River, Massachusetts)

fate in the form of another accident was to grant a reprieve to these attractive sisterships.

On January 2, 1935, *Lexington*, one of the two sister vessels of the Colonial Line, sank in the East River after being struck amidships by a freighter. The loss of *Lexington* left the Colonial Line (an overnight service between New York and Providence, Rhode Island, which since 1910 had dared to compete with the New Haven Railroad's steamship lines on Long Island Sound) short of steamers. For a year the line limped along by using its smaller spare steamer to run opposite *Concord*, *Lexington*'s surviving sistership, and by chartering a larger steamer from another line during the busier summer season. By 1935, even before the loss of *Lexington*, Colonial's executives had been looking for larger steamers for the run that could be secured at a reasonable price. When they found that *Belfast* and *Camden* had become available, they knew that these two steamers would be ideal for their route, as indeed they later proved to be. By June, 1936, all gleaming in fresh paint, *Belfast* and *Camden* had started their new service as *Arrow* and *Comet* on the daily overnight run of the Colonial Navigation Company out of New York and up Long Island Sound and

Narragansett Bay to Providence. It was also in 1936 that Peninsular and Occidental put *Belfast* and *Camden*'s contemporary, *Governor Cobb* (now thirty years old), up for sale. Over the two succeeding seasons, *Governor Cobb* reappeared in New England waters running between Boston and Provincetown. But she soon proved too large for the route and too expensive to operate. There were rumors in 1937 that the Colonial Line might buy *Governor Cobb* as a spare, since her turbine engines were virtually identical to those of the line's *Arrow* and *Comet*. But apparently the Colonial Line too was deterred by the size of her fuel bills. For a time in the late 1930s *Governor Cobb* was laid up in Philadelphia awaiting conversion to a trailer-carrier for a planned service which never materialized.

In 1936, the year that *Belfast* and *Camden* were sold, Eastern chartered *Iroquois*, one of the sisterships recently built for the the Clyde-Mallory Line's New York-Miami service, for the summer Portland route instead of *Florida*. *Iroquois* was fast enough to complete the usual two round trips per week between New York and Portland and also, on one of these trips, to continue from Portland on to Bar Harbor and

Advertisements for the inexpensive cruises run by Eastern Steamship in the 1930s during the Depression.

Comet, formerly *Camden* of Eastern's Boston-Bangor route, at her wharf in Providence, Rhode Island, shortly after she and her sistership *Belfast* had been sold to the Colonial Line in 1936. (R. Loren Graham Collection, Steamship Historical Society, University of Baltimore Library)

back at the northen end. Starting in 1937, as traffic on the route had begun to fall off, Eastern found it unnecessary to charter vessels from other lines and instead assigned the ever-accommodating *Acadia* to make one round trip per week between New York and Portland and one round trip between New York and Yarmouth.

With two pair of modern sisterships similar in style although differing in capacity, and with traffic demands shifting as a result both of the Depression and of growing reliance on private automobiles, Eastern tried many different scheduling patterns on its routes to Maine or Canada during the late 1930s, and ship assignments were changed almost, it would seem, at random. Consequently, although schedules for this era are available in company brochures, their frequent variations defy summarization.

On two occasions during the 1930s one of Eastern's ships was responsible for the loss of a smaller excursion steamer. At 5:30 P.M. on September 9, 1936, *New York* pulled away from India Wharf in Boston to start her regular overnight trip to New York, and, in spite of the thick fog, which was not unusual at that time of year, began threading her way among the is-

lands of Boston Harbor toward the open sea. Feeling her way into the harbor through the fog that evening was the excursion steamer *Romance* (formerly *Tennessee* of the Joy Line's New York-Providence route) returning from her day trip to Provincetown. As these two steamers approached each other in the fog off Gallop's Island, the officers of both steamers were aware that the other was near and were even in contact with each other by radio. Both steamers were also blowing their whistles at regular intervals. Nevertheless, *New York*'s pilot was completely surprised when *Romance* suddenly materialized through the mist barely a few yards dead ahead in his path.

Seconds later *New York* plowed into *Romance* and the smaller steamer began sinking immediately. Miraculously no one aboard *Romance* had been seriously injured. *New York* kept her bow wedged into the gash in the excursion steamer's side to keep her from going under until all passengers and crew had been safely taken aboard. Only when *Romance*'s captain, who was the last to leave his ship, was assured that there was no one left aboard, did *New York* back away. Apparently, when he saw *New York* approaching, the excursion steamer's pilot had tied down the

Comet, formerly Eastern Steamship's *Camden*: Interior view of Quarter Deck Entrance Hall, looking aft from starboard side after it had been redecorated in 1930s style by the Colonial Line. Swinging doors to the left opened to the Dining Saloon.

whistle cord, and apparently there was still steam in the boilers, for as *Romance* began to go down, her whistle was still blowing, and it continued its eerie bleating throughout the vessel's death throes until she finally slipped under.

After the accident *New York* returned to her wharf in Boston with the passengers from *Romance*. When a quick inspection revealed that *New York* had sustained virtually no injury in the encounter, she headed out once again, now about three hours behind schedule.

Less than two years later *Acadia* was involved in a strangely similar accident in New York harbor. On May 28, 1938, *Acadia* sailed from Pier #18 at 6:00 P.M., with the usual holiday farewell fanfare, on a special Memorial Day cruise to Bermuda, the kind

of cruise she often made in the weeks between her winter tour on the Boston run and her summer assignment running to Portland or Yarmouth. Although the skies were relatively clear when *Acadia* first pulled out of her pier into the North River, as she made her way down New York Harbor a thick fog began rolling in from the Atlantic, so that by the time she was passing through the Narrows, visibility for her pilots was virtually zero. That evening the 275-foot excursion steamer *Mandalay*, which made two daily round-trip runs between the Battery and Atlantic Highlands, New Jersey, was returning to Manhattan with 274 passengers aboard, many of them children. Apparently these passengers were in a holiday mood, because the newspapers reported that *Acadia*'s passengers could hear people singing aboard the excursion vessel before they

The excursion steamer *Romance*, formerly *Tennessee* of the Joy Line, was rammed and sunk by *New York* in Boston Harbor in 1936. (The Mariners Museum, Newport News, Virginia)

actually spotted her.

As the two vessels approached one another in the thickening fog, the captains of both vessels could hear the muffled whistle of the other, and both ordered their engines stopped. But with momentum and tide, Captain Cornning had no way to halt *Acadia*'s continuing movement, even when the crowded *Mandalay* suddenly materialized through the mist directly ahead of his ship. When *Acadia* crashed directly into the excursion vessel about amidships, Captain Cornning kept *Acadia*'s bow wedged into *Mandalay*'s side—as the captain of *New York* had with *Romance* just two years before—to keep her afloat as long as possible. Some of *Acadia*'s crew quickly rigged a makeshift gangplank between *Acadia*'s bow and *Mandalay*'s upper deck. Most of *Mandalay*'s passengers and crew of forty were able to climb to safety across this gangplank, although others were picked up from the water by the lifeboats *Acadia* lowered. Thanks to the professionalism of Captain Cornning and the crews of both vessels, no one was killed or even injured in the accident. Once it was assured that everyone had left the smaller vessel, and *Acadia* had backed away, *Mandalay* settled to the bottom in

about twenty minutes.

After the accident *Acadia* returned to her North River pier to discharge *Mandalay*'s passengers. An inspection ordered on the spot showed that *Acadia*'s sharp steel prow, both above and below the waterline, had sustained no damage other than scratched paint and a dent or two. Shortly after 10:00 that evening, *Acadia* sailed again. Her speed was sufficient to get her passengers to Bermuda on time for them to enjoy whatever shore trips the original schedule had promised.

Mandalay's owners (heirs of Charles Dimon, who by then was no longer living) shopped around over the next few days to find a large excursion steamer that could be made available immediately to take over the heavily travelled Atlantic Highlands route for that summer. Interestingly, the steamer they chartered was *Yankee*, formerly the familiar and much loved *J. T. Morse* of Eastern Steamship's line from Rockland to Mt. Desert, in Maine.

Although Eastern Steamship, with its new ocean-going vessels adapted to off-season cruising, and the Colonial Line, with its two older steamers purchased from Eastern which were relatively inex-

93

The excursion steamer *Mandalay* was rammed and sunk by *Acadia* in New York Harbor in 1938.

pensive to operate or maintain, had both been able to survive the Depression (and the automobile), during the mid-1930s the bankrupt New Haven Railroad was forced to give up its marine subsidiary, the New England Steamship Company. One by one this company's overnight steamship lines operating water-and-rail routes between New York and Boston in competition with Eastern's direct water route closed down. Finally in 1937 first the line to Providence and then the great Fall River Line itself stopped running. That fall all four of the Fall River Line's big sidewheel night boats were sold for scrap. Other than Eastern, only the smaller Colonial Line to Providence survived on Long Island Sound.

One might note that the enormous debt incurred by the New Haven Railroad in pursuing its virtually unbridled expansionist policy in the Morgan years before the First World War had never been amortized. Also, in spite of changing times and changing tastes in the 1920s and 1930s, the New England Steamship Company had made little effort to renew its fleet or even to modernize its ships. At the time the company closed down in 1937, only two of its eight passenger steamers had been built after the turn of the

century, and those two dated from before 1910. The two largest of the Fall River Line's steamers operated only during the heavy traffic months in summer, but had to be maintained through the rest of the year while two smaller steamers took over the route. Eastern Steamship, on the other hand, had dealt with its debt by selling its most valuable steamers in 1917, but as a result of the financial stability thus achieved and also of its far-sighted policy in establishing new routes, the company had been able in the era between 1924 and 1931 to produce a modern fleet well adapted to the rapidly changing demands of the travelling public in this era of automobiles.

With the closing of its Bangor line in 1935 and the sale of *Belfast* and *Camden* in 1936, Eastern Steamship had in little more than a decade produced not only a completely new fleet but also new routes and a new image. Before the First World War, Eastern Steamship had been essentially a collection of seasonal lines operating both wooden-hulled sidewheelers and a few more modern steel-hulled night boats on seasonal routes between Boston and ports along the coast of Maine. By 1936 all of the vessels serving on the routes of the Eastern Steamship Lines (save *Madi-*

son on the Old Dominion Line) were large new and modern ships built for the company since 1924: *Boston* and *New York*; *George Washington* and *Robert E. Lee*; *Evangeline* and *Yarmouth*; and *Acadia* and *Saint John*. All except *Boston* and *New York* were small ocean liners which could—and later did in war service—navigate almost anywhere in the world. All except *Boston* and *New York*, therefore, were capable of earning revenue throughout the year.

1. The American Bureau of Shipping, The American Merchant Marine, 1933, p. 14.

During the 1930s the inexpensive Easter Cruises to Bermuda aboard *Acadia* from New York or *Saint John* from Boston were especially popular.

VII. War and its Aftermath: 1939-1955

The summer of 1939 was an active one for the Eastern Steamship Lines. With many New Englanders heading for the exciting New York World's Fair that summer, *Boston* and *New York* were carrying more passengers than ever. The other routes too seemed to have recovered from any effects of the Depression that season. With *Acadia* running from New York to Portland or Yarmouth, *Saint John* from Boston to St. John, *Yarmouth* and *Evangeline* between Boston and Yarmouth, and *George Washington*, *Robert E. Lee*, and *Madison* between New York and Norfolk, Eastern Steamship was doing an excellent business. But events already brewing far from Boston were soon to bring an end to Eastern's good fortune.

On the first of September, 1939, the German Third Reich let loose a blitzkrieg invasion of Poland, its neighbor to the east. On September 3 Great Britain and France, both obligated by treaty to defend Poland, declared war on Germany. A week later many Americans attempting to flee from a Europe now at war were headed home aboard the British liner *Athenia* when she was torpedoed and sunk by a German submarine in the North Atlantic.

With the sinking of *Athenia*, the American government realized the necessity of sending as many American-flag ships as possible across the Atlantic immediately to evacuate American tourists and other Americans caught in Europe who would not have been safe crossing the ocean on a ship belonging to one of the belligerent nations, most of which had, in any event, cancelled their sailings. Late in September, therefore, scheduled cruises to Bermuda were cancelled on short notice when the 403-foot *Acadia* and *Saint John* were both among the ships ordered by the government to sail across the Atlantic for France, with large American flags hastily painted on their sides proclaiming their neutrality, to bring home stranded Americans. On her return from Europe, *Acadia* was caught in a hurricane. Some stalwart passengers, apparently accustomed to the luxuries of larger liners, later complained that *Acadia* had not continued serving full course meals during the hurricane. *Acadia*'s cooks countered that, with the ship tossing regularly

from a twenty degree angle in one direction to a twenty degree angle in the other direction, not to mention the intermittant pitching, they had not been able to keep vats of boiling edibles on their ranges. Disgruntled passengers notwithstanding, *Acadia* eventually arrived safely in New York, and was soon dispatched again, this time to South America to bring back State Department personnel as well as American tourists who had no return passage now that ships of European registries had been recalled for war duty.

The years 1939 and 1940 were busy times for Eastern's four newest liners. With Europe closed to tourists, Eastern's shorter winter and spring cruises to Bermuda, Nassau, or the Caribbean, as well as the line's regular summer services to Canada, were often fully booked. Much military traffic, now that the United States was beginning to bolster its own defense system in response to the war in Europe, also travelled on Eastern's vessels, particularly those of the Old Dominion Division which served the concentration of military bases in the Norfolk area.

After their return from Europe or South America, *Acadia* and *Saint John* again became, as usual at that time of year, Eastern Steamship's regular overnight boats between New York and Boston. Early in 1940, *Evangeline* sailed south on a short charter to the Seaboard Air Line Railroad, which for some reason wanted to use her to compete against Peninsular and Occidental's *Florida* on the overnight run between Miami and Havana that winter.

As soon as she was relieved on the Boston route in April, 1940, *Acadia* made several trips to Norfolk, while *Robert E. Lee* and *George Washington* went for their annual overhauls. That summer, since British ships could no longer service the Bahamas, *Saint John*, *Evangeline*, and *Yarmouth* alternated on the routes from Boston to Yarmouth and from New York to Portland and Yarmouth, while *Acadia* spent the season of 1940 sailing from New York every Saturday at 3:00 P.M. on a "Glorious Six-Day Cruise" to Nassau. When *Acadia* had to return to her New York-Boston route in the fall, Eastern continued the weekly service to Nassau through the winter with *Evangeline*.

Acadia when in service with Alcoa Lines in 1941. (Marine Museum at Fall River, Massachusetts)

The winter of 1940-1941 was to be the last for *Acadia* and *Saint John* on the New York-Boston route. These steamers had been constructed with federal loans under the terms of the Merchant Marine Act of 1928, and one of the stipulations had been that the federal government could take possession of them in a time of national emergency. Although the United States was still theoretically neutral, the government was aware that the country could become involved at any time, so that military preparations were necessary, and President Franklin D. Roosevelt had, without declaring war, declared a national emergency. In March, 1941, therefore, the government requisitioned both *Acadia* and *Saint John* for a mandatory charter to Alcoa Lines, so that *Boston* and *New York* had to relieve them on the New York-Boston route several weeks earlier than usual. Later that spring, both *Yarmouth* and *Evangeline* were taken for government service as well. *Yarmouth*'s last run from St. John to Boston in June, 1941, was to be the final trip of the former International Line, which had provided continuous service between Boston and St. John since before the Civil War. In their charters to Alcoa Eastern's ships were assigned to carry troops and sup-

plies to American bases in the Caribbean and to former British bases in Bermuda, the Bahamas, or the Caribbean recently transferred to the Americans in the "Lend-Lease" agreement. *Saint John*, as it turned out, had not even started on her new service with Alcoa before the government found it needed her for other purposes. In the spring of 1941 *Saint John* was sent instead to the shipyard to be rebuilt as a seaplane tender and renamed *Antaeus*, while *Evangeline* took over her assignment with Alcoa.

For the summer season of 1941, even before the United States had entered the war, all of Eastern's services to Canada (St. John or Yarmouth), Bermuda, or Nassau had to be cancelled. Eastern was able to maintain its freight service from both New York and Boston to Portland and from New York to Richmond for a short time longer. But with so many of its finest vessels in government service, the only passenger operations Eastern Steamship could offer in the 1941 season were with *Boston* and *New York* running between those cities and with *Robert E. Lee* and *George Washington* on the New York-Norfolk route.

Since there were no winter boats to relieve them, when *Boston* and *New York* ended their season on November 30, 1941, Eastern's New York-to-Boston service was simply suspended "until further notice." This was in fact the end for the New York-Boston line, a direct descendent of the Metropolitan Line, which had also been in continuous operation since the early 1860s, and of the passenger service inaugurated by Charles W. Morse with *Yale* and *Harvard* in September, 1907.

On December 7, 1941, just one week after *Boston* and *New York* had tied up for the season, the Japanese bombing of Pearl Harbor in Hawaii brought the United States with full force into the war. Among the American ships sunk that day at Pearl Harbor was the minelayer, U. S. S. *Oglala*, the former *Massachusetts* of Eastern Steamship's Metropolitan Line. After *Oglala* was subsequently raised and repaired, she continued to serve in the Pacific as a supply ship throughout the war, as did *Aroostook*, formerly *Bunker Hill*, her erstwhile running mate.

A short time later Eastern's small freight steamer *Cornish* was torpedoed and sunk in the Atlantic, the first American vessel to become a victim of German U-boats.

After Pearl Harbor and the subsequent declaration of war by both Germany and Italy, the United States found itself with an inadequate merchant fleet while involved in a bitterly faught conflict on two oceans. With its urgent need to transport troops, armaments, and other supplies to Europe, to Africa, to islands in the Pacific, and even to Russia, as well as to bring rubber and other necessities from Latin America into the United States, the government began to gather any vessels it could find that could do these jobs, and even many that in peacetime would have seemed utterly unsuited, but which in this emergency could somehow be adapted for the work to be done. As a result, the staunchly-built ocean-going ships of the Eastern Steamship Lines, although very small compared with most ocean-going passenger vessels, were very much in demand. Every one of them was called to serve the country in this emergency, and many of these vessels, although some had been designed mainly for overnight services along the coast of Maine, travelled over the next three years to distant parts of the world in all kinds of seas and in all kinds of weather.

Once the United States had entered the war, the Old Dominion ships, *George Washington*, *Robert E. Lee*, and *Madison* (renamed *Warzsawa*, the Polish spelling for Warsaw, during her military service) were also requisitioned for government service. *George Washington* and *Robert E. Lee* were turned over to Alcoa Lines. With American ships in the Atlantic being sunk by German submarines, often not many miles off the coast, Eastern Steamship could not have maintained the New York-to-Norfolk service in any event. During December, 1941, as the United States rapidly girded for the crisis, even *Boston* and *New York*— which had also been built with government loans— were taken for war duty. *Boston* was sent to New London, Connecticut, to serve as a barracks for a Merchant Marine training center hastily set up there. *New York* was used for a similar purpose at Thompkinsville on Staten Island in New York.

By 1942 Eastern Steamship Lines had no vessels at all in service. But the company remained active throughout the war managing troopships and cargo vessels—supplying crews, fueling, or arranging itineraries—under contract with the government.

Early in 1942 the Colonial Line's *Arrow* and *Comet*, formerly *Belfast* and *Camden* of Eastern's Boston-Bangor Division, were also requisitioned for military service. *Arrow*'s last trip from Providence to New York in March, 1942, marked the end of overnight passenger steamers on Long Island Sound, where a mere eleven years before a dozen overnight steamers had left each port every night. Interestingly, these two steamers, whose hulls had been considered too fragile to be licensed for the route between Boston and Bangor, Maine, only seven years before, were now completely rebuilt from the guards up and dispatched under their own power from New York to Hawaii, where they spent the war years ferrying troops and supplies among the islands. Their contemporary, *Governor Cobb*, saw military service during the war as well. Renamed U. S. S. *Cobb*, she was assigned to Coast Guard duty in the Atlantic.

In June, 1942, the government took *Acadia* from her service with Alcoa and sent her up to Boston, where she was converted into a "Hospital Transport" vessel, which apparently meant that she was part hospital ship and part troop carrier. With this double designation she did not qualify for the immunities granted to Hospital Ships by The Hague Convention. [1]

Yarmouth was assigned to take *Acadia*'s place on Alcoa's routes, but she was not to remain long in this service. During the summer of 1942, Alcoa relinquished *Yarmouth* and *Evangeline* to the government, and both were to spend the war years as military transports. With the departure of *Yarmouth* and

Evangeline as a troopship during the Second World War. (U. S. Army Signal Corps Photograph)

Comet, formerly *Camden* of Eastern Steamship, her conversion for military service completed at the Army's docks in Brooklyn in 1942, ready to sail with her sistership, *Arrow*, to Hawaii.
(U. S. Army Signal Corps Photograph)

The submarine tender, *Antaeus*, formerly Eastern Steamship's *Saint John*, in service during the Second World War.

Evangeline, Alcoa assigned *George Washington* and *Robert E. Lee* to their duties supplying bases in Bermuda, Nassau, and the Caribbean. On July 30, 1942, *Robert E. Lee*, returning to New Orleans from a supply run to bases in the Caribbean, was torpedoed and sunk in the Gulf of Mexico, only fifty miles from the mouth of the Mississippi.

Alcoa Lines continued operating her sistership, *George Washington*, on these routes for the duration of the war. On one occasion when *George Washington* was sent to Trinidad to pick up a contingent of soldiers, her officers were suprised to find over 4,000 troops at the wharf waiting to board her. They eventually discovered that they had mistakenly received an order intended for the large former German ocean liner, *George Washington* (the ship that had taken Woodrow Wilson to France in 1918), then also serving as an American troop transport.

One might have expected that Eastern's ocean-going passenger vessels, even though they were comparatively small, would be called upon to serve their country on the high seas in various parts of the world in this time of national emergency. But there could also have been a reasonable assumption that *Boston* and *New York*, which had been built solely for a summer service in protected waters, would probably best be utilized where they were, as barracks ships in New London and Staten Island. There was some confusion, therefore, and even disbelief, when in the late summer of 1942 *Boston* and *New York* were ordered to proceed to a shipyard to have their superstructures reinforced in preparation for joining a trans-Atlantic convoy.

On their arrival in St. Johns, Newfoundland, where the convoy was to assemble, *Boston* and *New York*, as it turned out, did not find themselves the only coastal-type steamers in a convoy of larger ocean-going vessels. On the contrary, *Boston* and *New York* were by far the largest vessels in a convoy consisting entirely of American inland water steamers. Largest among the other ships was the much smaller *President Warfield*, the overnight steamer from Chesapeake Bay which had run as an extra boat with *Boston* and *New York* under charter in 1930. Also among the steamers there assembled were *Northland* and *Southland*, 300-foot overnight steamers that had run on the Potomac River between Washington and Norfolk, both dating from before the First World War, and *Yorktown*, an even smaller though newer vessel, also from Chesapeake Bay. Although *Boston* and *New York* had been built with steel hulls and steel shells around their superstructures, all of the other vessels mentioned, while they also had steel hulls, were built entirely of wood above the guards. Rounding out this strange convoy were *Naushon* and *New Bedford*, small day steamers from the line that ran from New Bedford, Massachusetts, out to the offshore islands of Martha's Vineyard and Nantucket.

Even among those few people who knew of the existence of this convoy at the time, there seems to have been little agreement about its intended function. One version asserts that the convoy was intended only as a decoy to draw German submarines away from another more strategically significant convoy. It is possible that the convoy was indeed designed to lure German U-Boats into remaining active in the North Atlantic at the time when the United States was planning a massive movement of troops across the Atlantic farther south for the invasion of North Africa. Whether or not the convoy was to serve partly as a decoy, it is also true that, with the Normandy invasion already in planning stages, the Allies foresaw the necessity of sending as many light-draft vessels across to Great Britain as possible.

With most experienced American mariners on more crucial assignments at this time, it proved difficult to find a crew willing to risk taking these small coastal steamers across the sub-infested Atlantic. As it was a private British company that finally agreed to man these steamers and accept the risk of piloting them across the ocean, all of the vessels in the convoy were transferred to British registry. The British Navy also supplied two destroyers to accompany the convoy. On September 23, 1942, this "skimming dish fleet," as some chose to call it, departed from St. Johns and steamed out into the Atlantic. For the first two days the convoy saw no evidence of enemy submarines. Then on September 25, at 2:30 in the afternoon, *Boston* was struck by two torpedoes forward on the port side. According to witnesses on other vessels, *Boston* sank in about four minutes. The few survivors were picked up by one of the destroyers or by *New Bedford*.

About 9:00 that evening *New York* was also hit by torpedoes. She burst into flames, and then she too went under. One of the British destroyers was sunk in the same attack, and *Yorktown* was also later torpedoed, but somehow all of the other small American steamers in this "riverboat" convoy eventually made their way to some safe harbor either in Ireland or Scotland and survived to serve in other roles in the war.

Shortly after both *Boston* and *New York* had been sunk in the North Atlantic, *Evangeline* was to cross the Atlantic as part of the larger convoy carrying American troops to Morrocco for the African Campaign. Once the invasion had started, *Evangeline* made several more crossings taking troops and supplies to various Mediterranean ports in North Africa.[2]

Acadia also took part in the African Campaign. As a combined troopship-hospital ship, *Acadia* was to make three round trips to North Africa, carrying troops across and returning with wounded in the fall of 1942 and early 1943. Later in 1943 *Acadia* was again somewhat modified to operate solely as a Hospital Ship, and in this role she was to serve primarily in the Pacific for the duration of the war. *Antaeus* (a. *Saint John*) was also converted into a Hospital Ship in 1943, but, whereas *Acadia* as a Hospital Ship was not much changed internally from her days as a passenger vessel, *Antaeus* had already been so altered that it was clear she would never again operate as a passenger ship.

During 1942 and 1943, while *Acadia* and *Evangeline* were plying the warm seas of the Mediterranean, *Yarmouth*, operating mainly out of Boston, was carrying troops and supplies to bases in Newfoundland, Laborador, and Greenland. By 1944, however, both *Yarmouth* and *Evangeline* had been transferred to the Pacific where they remained as troop carriers for the duration of the war.[3]

When the war finally ended in 1945, only *Yarmouth* and *Evangeline* were returned to Eastern Steamship Lines. As we have noted, before the United States had been involved in the war for a year, three of the nine passenger vessels contributed by Eastern, *Robert E. Lee*, *Boston*, and *New York*, had been torpedoed and sunk by German U-Boats. The only Eastern Steamship freighters to survive the war were *Sandwich* and *Falmouth*, but they were both sold by the government to other operators after the war. *Saint John*, as we have seen, had been so altered for military service that she was no longer suited for peacetime service. *Acadia*, *George Washington*, and *Madison* had all survived, but none of the three were ever returned to Eastern. In 1946, with her war duty as a hospital ship over, *Acadia* returned to San Francisco, where she was again converted, this time to a troopship to bring servicemen and dependants back from military assignments in the Pacific.

By 1948 *Acadia* had returned from the Pacific to Norfolk, and the government was prepared to transfer her back to Eastern Steamship Lines. When the Newport News Shipbuilding and Drydock Co. gave Eastern an estimate of $5,000,000 for reconverting *Acadia* to peacetime passenger service, Eastern claimed that the Maritime Commission had to pay the line enough to cover the reconversion of its ship. The Commission took the position, however, that according to the terms of the Merchant Marine Act of 1928, the government was obliged to pay Eastern only the estimated value of the ship at the time she was requisitioned, which was perhaps less than half that amount. While Eastern and the government attempted, eventually unsuccessfully, to reach a mutually agreeable settlement, *Acadia* sat for nearly a decade in lay-up in Norfolk, where, according to the New York *Herald Tribune*, she was "more securely tied by legal red tape than by her hawsers." Since Eastern was not in a position to pay for her reconstruction without more compensation than the government was offering, the beautiful *Acadia*, still a relatively new ship, was ultimately scrapped.

Warzsawa (a. *Madison*) was also scrapped in 1948.

In March, 1945, shortly before the war ended, Eastern, for some reason, sold *George Washington* to the War Shipping Adminsitration, which maintained the charter to Alcoa. When she was released from her military duties in 1946, Alcoa continued to operate her between New York and Bermuda for two years until the British ship usually assigned to this service had been rebuilt and returned to the route. Early in 1948 the government sold *George Washington* to the Alaska Transportation Company to revive the service between Seattle and Alaska. When this company encountered first the inflated costs of repairs and then a series of strikes, it sold *George Washington* after only one season to the French Line, which renamed her *Gascogne* and operated her on a route between LeHavre and the French West Indies. This too was a temporary assignment on which she was to serve only until the French Line's larger ship, *Columbie*, assigned to this service, completed her post-war reconversion. After about a year with the French Line, *Gascogne* was transferred to the Messageries Maritimes, the French steamship company operating between Marseilles and French Indo-China (primarily to Viet-Nam). According to fairly reliable reports, *Gascogne* (a. *George Washington*) was scrapped in Hong Kong in the fall of 1955, at which time, although she had by then served in many parts of the world, she was still just over thirty years old.

Several of the former Eastern Steamship vessels had also survived the war. U. S. S. *Cobb* (a. *Governor Cobb*) returned at the end of the war and was tied up for some time among the vessels in the James River reserve fleet, but she was later scrapped. *Arrow*

(a. *Belfast*) returned from Hawaii after the war but was wrecked by being blown ashore on the coast of Washington while under tow. One of her masts still stands, however, as a flagpole somewhere on the Oregon Coast. Her sistership, *Comet* (a. *Camden*), was sold to run on the Yangtse River in China, where, according to unreliable reports, she was scrapped about 1955, by which time she would have been in service for forty-eight years.

U. S. S. *Aroostook* (a. *Bunker Hill*) managed two interesting post scripts to her career after the war. Even before the war ended, *Aroostook*, docked in Seattle, had been declared unfit for further service, sold for scrap, and towed away. Government agents, therefore, were somewhat baffled shortly after the war ended to discover this vessel, renamed (though not officially) *Lux*, operating illegally as a gambling vessel several miles off the coast of Los Angeles. After she was siezed by the government, *Aroostook* was later towed to the Bikini atoll in the Pacific to participate in the Atomic bomb tests performed there. It would seem safe to assume that these tests were sufficiently successful to account for her permanent demise.

Although only two (out of nine) passenger ships (*Yarmouth* and *Evangeline*) were returned to Eastern Steamship after the war, the government eventually paid the company $5,185,000 as restitution for its losses. This amount barely covered the cost of reconditioning the two vessels returned. It certainly did not come close to allowing Eastern Steamship to build new ships and re-establish the routes it had operated before the war. In a sense, however, even with only two ships available, Eastern Steamship was in a better position after the war than most of the other companies which had operated on routes along the Atlantic coast before their ships were requisitioned for war service. Many companies with similar operations, such as the Ocean Steamship Company (Savannah Line), the Clyde-Mallory Line, the New York and Cuba Mail (Ward) Line, the New York and Porto Rico Line, the Merchants and Miners Line, or the Colonial Line, were not able to re-establish their services at all after the war. In most cases their ships had been lost during the conflict or had been so altered for military service (not to mention badly used) that any reconversion was either impossible or too expensive to contemplate. Although the government was reasonably generous in granting compensation for vessels requisitioned in the emergency, by the time some of the ships were returned to their owners, the costs of yard

Of Eastern's Pre-War Fleet, only *Yarmouth* resumed regular service after the War.
(Marine Museum at Fall River, Massachusetts)

work, of crews, and of general maintenance had escalated to the point that reconverting their ships was prohibitive and building new vessels out of the question. Eastern was among the few even to try to employ their returned vessels on pre-war routes. Virtually all of the other major companies that had operated between American ports on the Atlantic Coast before the war simply went out of business.

Yarmouth and *Evangeline* were returned to Eastern Steamship in February, 1946, six months after the end of the war. It was to take over a year, however, to have them reconverted for peacetime service. The cost of reconditioning *Evangeline* alone, at Bethlehem Steel's yard in Quincy, Massachusetts, came to $1,500,000, or about what it had cost to build her originally twenty years before.[4]

With only *Yarmouth* and *Evangeline* returned to the company, and the possibility of renewing its fleet by building new ships ruled out by post-war prices, only the Boston-Yarmouth route was revived. None of Eastern's other services—the Boston-St. John, Boston-New York, New York-Portland, New York-Yarmouth, or New York-Norfolk routes—could be resumed after the war.

Yarmouth was the first to be ready for peacetime service. Starting on February 28, 1947, Eastern Steamship's first post-war operation was to send *Yarmouth* on a series of one-week cruises from New York to Nassau. Then on Memorial Day weekend of 1947 *Yarmouth* made her first sailing on the revived Boston-Yarmouth route. *Yarmouth* remained alone on the route, however, and offered sailings from each port only three times a week. Considering the greatly increased costs of fuel, maintenance, and crews after the war, Eastern was soon to discover that the profits of operating even one steamer on the Yarmouth route were minimal. Only a substantial subsidy from the Canadian government, eager to promote trade and tourism to Nova Scotia, made it possible for Eastern to maintain even this curtailed service.

By June, 1947, *Evangeline*'s reconversion had also been completed, but rather than place her on the Yarmouth run with her sistership, Eastern sent her on weekly cruises from New York to Bermuda. By midsummer, however, Eastern was finding that the combination of *Evangeline*'s poor performance, as a result of four years of war duty in two oceans with minimal maintenance, and the higher post-war costs of

104

fuel and labor, had rendered the operation of this beautiful steamer unprofitable. In August, therefore, Eastern cancelled the Bermuda cruises, and the recently reconditioned *Evangeline* spent the next several years idle at Pier #18 in Manhattan.

Throughout these years there were many rumors about possible services for *Evangeline*. By 1950 Eastern had developed fairly firm plans to place her on a revived New York-Norfolk run.[5] But just as these plans were taking shape a seamen's strike was able to gain a settlement which included not only significantly higher wages but also a guarantee of more suitable quarters for crews aboard American-flag vessels. Difficult financially as these awards were to be for the few surviving American steamship companies, especially those accustomed to pre-war operating methods, improved quarters were a benefit members of the American Merchant Marine certainly deserved and should have been awarded a century earlier. Before these provisions were granted, crew's quarters on most American (or other) vessels had often been abominable, sometimes dark and crowded areas occupied by several crewmen together in the vulnerable and windowless bowels of the vessel.

For Eastern, however, these regulations rendered the operation of its steamers even less profitable, since the new requirements meant placing crew members in sections of the ship that had previously served as revenue-producing passenger quarters. As a result, plans to operate *Evangeline* to Norfolk were dropped, and the line gave serious thought to abandoning the summer Yarmouth route as well.

In the end Eastern Steamship simply circumvented the new regulations by removing their steamers from American registry. In 1950 both *Yarmouth* and *Evangeline* were registered in Liberia, a country known for its lax regulations and its indifference either to the conditions of its crews or or to the safety of its passengers. With this foreign registry, *Evangeline* would not have been allowed to run between New York and Norfolk, as foreign-flag ships are not permitted to carry paying passengers between two American ports. Only because, on her summer run to Yarmouth and on her winter cruises to Bermuda or Nassau, *Yarmouth* was plying between an American port and a foreign port, was the Liberian loophole permissible, if perhaps even then not ethically justifiable.

At the end of the 1953 season, with profits still disappointing, Eastern was not able to resist an attractive offer for *Yarmouth*. Early in 1954 *Yarmouth* was sold to Frank Leslie Fraser for $500,000.[5] Fraser changed the vessel's name to *Yarmouth Castle*, which for some reason he considered more appropriate for a cruise vessel, and her registry to Panama, another country with notoriously lax requirements either for crews or for safety. It also allowed him to hire foreign crews, for whom he was not obliged to provide either the wages or the quarters guaranteed to American crews. Apparently in an effort to fool the public into believing that the ship was still operated by her more prestigious former owners, Fraser named his cruise outfit "Eastern Shipping Corporation."

In Fraser's service *Yarmouth Castle* alternated between nine-day cruises from Miami to Jamaica and Haiti, and four-day cruises from Miami to Nassau and Havana. After her first season *Yarmouth Castle*'s hull was painted white, as was then the fashion among cruise ships. Unfortunately, in this all-white livery she was never as attractive as she had been with her black hull when in the service of Eastern Steamship.

With *Yarmouth* sold, for the season of 1954 Eastern placed *Evangeline* on the Boston-Yarmouth run. By this time, however, it was becoming clear that the route was no longer profitable. In 1954 the Canadian government, disappointed with the short season offered by Eastern's service, had withdrawn its subsidy and instead inaugurated a line of its own, with a brand new vessel, between Bar Harbor and Yarmouth. *Evangeline*'s trip from Yarmouth to Boston on September 19, 1954, was the last sailing of the Eastern Steamship Lines, the descendant of the company founded over half a century earlier by Charles Wyman Morse. By the time her season on the Yarmouth route ended, Eastern had already agreed to sell *Evangeline* to Frank Fraser, the Miami cruise operator who had purchased *Yarmouth* earlier that year. The reason Fraser needed another vessel for his cruise service was that in the fall of 1954 he had concluded a two-year contract with the government of Nassau to operate *Yarmouth Castle* on regular cruises offering two round trips per week between Miami and Nassau. This contract included the stipulation that *Yarmouth Castle* be renamed *Queen of Nassau* while she was in this service.[6]

After some modifications necessary to prepare her for her new role, the first of several, *Evangeline* sailed south in November, 1954, to take over her sistership's cruise routes. When in 1956 her contract with the government of Nassau had expired, *Queen of Nassau,* again renamed *Yarmouth Castle,* joined *Evangeline* in offering cruises out of Miami.

Over the next several years the two sisterships were transferred to a variety of different cruise lines and assigned to a variety of routes. Between 1957 and 1959, for instance, first *Yarmouth Castle* and then *Evangeline* also offered cruises to Nassau out of Washington, D.C. In 1962 *Yarmouth Castle* was sent to the West Coast on a charter to operate between San Francisco and the Seattle World's Fair of that year. Since she was still registered in Panama, however, she could not run between two American ports. Thus *Yarmouth Castle* sailed from San Francisco to Vancouver, where her passengers had to transfer to a Canadian vessel for the trip back down to Seattle. For the most part, however, both *Evangeline* and *Yarmouth Castle,* every year appearing shabbier, were employed on relatively cheap cruises out of Miami.

On one occasion in 1964, *Yarmouth Castle* was scheduled for a special cruise out of New York, when at the last minute it was found she was not in condition to sail, and *Evangeline* was readied to make the cruise in her place. Since passengers and travel agencies had contracted for a cruise aboard "*Yarmouth Castle,*" that ship's name was hastily restored to "*Yarmouth,*" and the name "*Yarmouth Castle*" assigned to *Evangeline.*[7] To the confusion of both passengers and marine reporters, so the names remained.

On the afternoon of Friday, November, 12, 1965, *Yarmouth Castle* (the former *Evangeline*), by then back on her Miami-Nassau run, steamed out through the Miami channel on one of her regular three-day cruises to Nassau. Shortly after midnight fire broke out in an unused cabin and spread rapidly. The series of horrors and evidences of blatant incompetence on the part of her crew that ensued were eerily reminiscent of the *Morro Castle* fire of thirty-one years before. Efforts to extinguish the fire proved futile when hardly any of the hoses were found to be in working order (illustrating just one of the dangers of allowing vessels registered in Panama or Liberia to solicit American passengers or to schedule sailings out of American ports). As the fire began to rage rapidly out of control, it seemed not to occur to any of the crew to awaken sleeping passengers. And, since the cabin where the fire had started was located directly beneath the radio shack, the radio operator on duty was early forced to flee from his post, and the fiercely burning *Yarmouth Castle* had no way to send radio messages either to other ships or to the Coast Guard.

Fortunately other vessels in the area, notably *Bahama Star* of a competing cruise line to Nassau, and *Finnpulp,* a Finnish freighter, saw the flames and sped to the side of the burning *Yarmouth Castle.* When the first lifeboat from *Yarmouth Castle* to reach *Finnpulp* contained mainly crew members including several officers (and according to one report, the captain!), the appalled Finnish master refused to take them aboard and instead ordered the crew members in the boat to return to *Yarmouth Castle* and to assume their responsibility in assisting passengers trying to escape from the conflagration.

When *Yarmouth Castle* finally capsized and sank shortly after six the following morning, eighty-nine people were dead. Most had died in the flames. It is not known how many lost their lives in the shark-infested waters of the Bahamas. And so ended the career of *Yarmouth Castle,* the former *Evangeline* of the Eastern Steamship Lines, one of the most attractive and most beloved steamships ever operated in American waters.

Following the loss of her sistership, *Yarmouth* continued in the Miami-Nassau cruise service for another year, but bookings were so poor, understandably, that she was retired in 1966. After two years in lay-up *Yarmouth* was sold to a Greek concern which renamed her *Elizabeth A.* and announced plans to employ her on cruise routes in the Mediterranean. *Yarmouth* never operated on Mediterranean cruises, however. Instead, her new owners simply sent her to that limbo of floating hulks the Greeks maintain at Elefsis.

In 1955, after selling *Yarmouth* and *Evangeline,* the only remaining vessels in its fleet, the directors of the Eastern Steamship Lines, Incorporated, elected to dissolve the company. Symbolically, the vast India Wharf in Boston, from which most of Eastern Steamship's vessels had departed for their various destinations, burned in 1955.

1. Rowland W. Charles, <u>Troopships of World War II</u>, The Army Transportation Assosiation, Washington, 1947, p. 3.
2. *Ibid.,* p. 23.
3. *Ibid.,* p. 66.
4. Eisele, "*Saga of the Surviving Coastal Twins*", pp. 209-16.
5. *Ibid.*
6. *Ibid.*
7. *Ibid.*

Major Vessels of Eastern Steamship and Metropolitan Line: 1901-1955

Note: As a rule, the length given is "Length between Perpendiculars," and the beam given is the beam of hull. Since many of the vessels of Eastern Steamship were of the inland water type, with superstructures wider than their hulls and often longer as well, these figures do not always provide the information desired. Where known, therefore, the overall length and overall beam are given below as well in parentheses.

Acadia

Dimensions:	387.4(403)x61x22.5
Tonnage:	Gross, 6185
Hull:	Steel
Engine:	Twin-screw geared turbines
Horsepower:	14,250

1931-1932:	Built at Newport News Shipbuilding and Dry Dock Co. with sistership, *Saint John*, for Eastern Steamship Lines
1932-1941:	Served on various routes for Eastern Steamship, mainly as a winter boat for its New York-Boston service and on summer routes from New York to Portland or Yarmouth. Also made between-season cruises from New York or Boston to Bermuda or Nassau.
1939:	Special trip to France to evacuate Americans from Europe at war; special trip to South America to bring back stranded Americans
1941:	Requisitioned by U. S. government for mandated charter to Alcoa Lines to operate to bases in the Caribbean
1942:	Converted to combination troop transport/hospital ship and served essentially between the United States and North Africa
1943-1945:	Converted to Hospital Ship and served mainly in the Pacific
1945-1946:	Troop transport bringing servicemen in Pacific areas back to the United States
1946-1952:	In lay-up in Norfolk, Virginia. Government prepared to return her to Eastern Steamship. As the government did not offer enough compensation to pay for her proper reconversion for peacetime service, Eastern did not accept delivery.
c. 1953:	Scrapped

Bay State

Dimensions:	281.2x42.1x15,5
Tonnage:	Gross, 2262; Net, 1555 (Before 1909; new tonnage apparently not registered after 1909)
Hull:	Wood
Engine:	Sidewheel, walking-beam
Horsepower:	1200

1895:	Built by New England Shipbuilding Company, Bath, Maine, for Portland Steam Packet Co. (Boston-Portland overnight route)
1895-1898:	Ran opposite sistership *Portland* (built, 1890; lost 1898) on Boston-Portland overnight route
1899-1908:	Boston-Portland route opposite *Governor Dingley*
1901:	Portland Line became part of Eastern Steamship Company
1909:	International route, Boston-St. John
1909-1910:	Stripped to the guards and rebuilt with greater passenger capacity.
1910-1916:	Boston-Portland opposite *Ransom B. Fuller*
1916:	September 24: Aground at Cape Elizabeth, Maine. Blown apart in subsequent storm.

Belfast (b. Arrow)

Dimensions: 320.6(332)x40(54)x16.1
Tonnage: Gross, 2157; Net, 1147
Hull: Steel
Engine: Triple-screw direct-acting Parsons turbines
Horsepower: 4000

1909:   Built at Bath Iron Works, Bath, Maine, for Boston and Bangor Division of Eastern Steamship Co.
1909-1917:   Ran opposite sistership Camden on Boston and Bangor Division
1918-1919:   Substituted on Metropolitan Line, New York-Boston
1920-1935:   Boston-Bangor route oppposite sistership, Camden
1936:   April: Sold, with sistership Camden to Colonial Navigation Co.; renamed Arrow
1936-1942:   On Colonial Line's overnight route between New York and Providence, Rhode Island
1942:   Requisitioned by U. S. Army for war service; taken to Brooklyn Army docks; stripped to the guards and rebuilt for military service; sailed under her own power to Hawaii
1942-1945:   Served with sistership, Comet (a. Camden), as supply ship and military transport among Hawaian Islands
1947:   While under tow headed south along Pacific coast, caught in a storm, broke away from tow, forced ashore and foundered near Long Beach, Washington

Boothbay (b. Grampus, c. Deepwater)

Dimensions: 126x33x10
Tonnage: Gross, 334; Net, 224
Hull: Iron
Engine: Single-screw, reciprocating
Horsepower: 600

1907:   Built in Philadelphia as a day boat between Bath and Boothbay Harbor
1909:   Proved too large for Kennebec route; transferred to Penobscot Bay
1913-1931:   In government service; renamed Grampus
1932:   Operated by private interests in Norfolk, Virginia, as Boothbay
1933:   Sold to Virginia Navigation Co.; renamed Deepwater
1938:   Sold to McAllister Navigation Co. to run from Battery in Manhattan to Coney Island
1939:   Sold back to Virginia Navigation Co., then to Sutton Lines in New York
1939-1942:   Battery-Statue of Liberty boat for Sutton Lines
1942:   To U. S. government for war service

Boston

Dimensions: 384.3(402)x50(72.5)x20
Tonnage: Gross, 4989
Hull: Steel
Engines: Twin-screw geared turbines
Horsepower: 7600

1924:   Built with sistership, New York, at Bethlehem Steel yard at Sparrows Point, Maryland
1924-1941:   Summer service, opposite New York on Eastern Steamship's New York-Boston route
1941-1942:   Barracks ship for Merchant Martine training school at New London, Connecticut
1942:   August: Strengthened, armed, and painted gray for assignment overseas
1942:   Sept. 23: Joined convoy of inland water vessels destined for Great Britain
1942:   Sept. 25: Torpedoed and sunk in Atlantic

Brandon (b. *Yonda L.*, c. *Riviere du Loup*, d. *Simeon*)

Dimensions:	200.5x37x17.3
Tonnage:	Gross, 1062; Net 639
Hull:	Steel
Engines:	Single-screw, reciprocating
Horsepower:	1200

1902:	Built with sistership, *Berkeley*, at Harlan and Hollingsworth for Old Dominion Steamship Company
1902-1920:	Ran Norfolk-Richmond for Old Dominion
1920-1925:	Laid up
1923:	Old Dominion sold to Eastern Steamship
1925-1928:	Various routes on Maine coast for Eastern Steamship
1929:	Sold for service on St. Lawrence River; name changed successively to *Yonda L.*, *Riviere du Loup*, and *Simeon*
1938:	Abandoned at Quebec

Bunker Hill (b. U. S. S. *Aroostook*, c. *Lux*)

Dimensions:	375x52.2x30.2
Tonnage:	Gross, 4779; Net, 2575 (although not clear at which phase these measurements were taken)
Hull:	Steel
Engines:	Twin-screw, reciprocating, triple-expansion
Horsepower:	7000

1907:	Built at William Cramp and Son, Philadelphia, with sisterships *Massachusetts* and *Old Colony* first as a freighter for the New England Steamship Company (subsidiary of New Haven Railroad) to compete on the New York-Boston around-the-cape route against the Metropolitan Line's *Yale* and *Harvard*
1910-1911:	Passenger accommodations added and fuel changed to oil when New Haven RR decided to operate these ships on a passenger and cargo route New York-Boston, after Metropolitan sold *Yale* and *Harvard*
1911-1917:	Operated with sistership, *Massachusetts*, on New York-Boston passenger and freight service for Eastern Steamship; passenger accommodations considerably increased in 1912
1916:	Route changed to operate through the Cape Cod Canal
1917-1945:	In U. S. Navy as Minelayer, U.S.S. *Aroostook*
1945-1946:	Supposedly sold for scrap, secretly served briefly as gambling ship unofficially renamed *Lux* off California coast; discovered and repossessed by government
1947:	Towed to Bikini to be used and destroyed in atom bomb tests

Calvin Austin

Dimensions:	298(322)x60(o.a.)x17.8
Tonnage:	Gross, 3826; Net, 2853
Hull:	Steel
Engines:	Single screw, reciprocating, triple-expansion
Horsepower:	2700

1903:	Built at John Roach's Yard Chester, Pennsylvania, for the International Division of Eastern Steamship Company
1903-1917:	On Eastern's International Division: Boston, Portland, Eastport, Lubec, St. John, N.B.
1918:	Merchant Marine Training Ship
1919-1923:	Summer service of Metropolitan Line (New York-Boston) of Eastern Steamship Co.
1924:	International Division
1925:	New York-Portland
1926:	International Division
1927-1928:	Boston-Portland
1929-1931:	International Division
1931:	Out of service at end of season
1933:	Sold for scrap

Camden (b. Comet)

Dimensions:	320(332.6)x40(54)x16.1
Tonnage:	2153 Gross; 1143 Net
Hull:	Steel
Engine:	Triple-screw direct-acting Parsons turbines
Horsepower:	4000

1907:	Built at Bath Iron Works, Bath, Maine, for Boston and Bangor Division of Eastern Steamship Co.
1907:	Boston-Bangor route
1908:	International route: Boston-Saint John
1909-1917:	Boston-Bangor route opposite sistership, *Belfast*
1918:	Boston-New York route opposite sistership, *Belfast*
1919:	Boston-Bangor route opposite *City of Bangor*
1920-1935:	Boston-Bangor route opposite sistership, *Belfast*
1936:	April: Sold with sistership *Belfast* to Colonial Navigation Co.; renamed *Comet*
1936-1942:	On Colonial Line's overnight route between New York and Providence, Rhode Island
1942:	Requisitioned by U. S. Army for war service; taken to Army docks in Brooklyn, stripped to the guards; rebuilt for military service; sailed to Hawaii
1942-1945:	Military transport and supply ship among Hawaian Islands with sistership *Arrow* (a. *Belfast*)
1948:	Sold for service in China
1955:	Reported scrapped in China

City of Augusta (b. *St. Johns*)

Dimensions:	150x31.3x6.5
Tonnage:	Gross, 330; Net, 252
Hull:	Wood
Engines:	Sternwheel
Horsepower:	300

1906:	Built in Boston for the Kennebec Division of Eastern Steamship
1906-1915:	Connected with overnight steamer to Boston at Bath and carried transferred passengers and cargo from Bath to landings upriver as far as Augusta
1915-1917:	Laid up
1917-1918:	Sold and renamed *St. Johns*; operated on St. Johns River ferrying workers from Jacksonville to nearby wartime shipyard
c. 1919:	Sold to become floating nightclub in Savannah, Georgia
c. 1922:	Burned at Savannah

City of Bangor

Dimensions:	277x38x14.2
Tonnage:	Gross, 1161; Net, 1113
Hull:	Wood
Engine:	Sidewheel, walking-beam
Horsepower:	1600

1894:	Built in Boston for Boston and Bangor Steamship Company to replace *Katahdin* of 1864
1894-1906:	Ran between Boston and Bangor, with stops at Rockland and other landings along the Penobscot
1901:	Boston and Bangor Steamship Co. became part of the Eastern Steamship Company
1907:	Boston-Kennebec River
1908:	Boston-Bangor
1909-1917:	Boston-Kennebec River
1913:	Burned at Boston and considerably rebuilt
1918:	Boston-Bangor
1919-1922:	Boston-Portland
1923-1925:	Boston-Kennebec River
1926-1927:	Boston-Portland
1927:	Laid up in East Boston at end of season
1933:	Sank in East Boston and abandoned

City of Rockland

Dimensions:	274.3xx38.5x14.4
Tonnage:	Gross, 1696; Net, 1026
Hull:	Wood
Engine:	Sidewheel, walking-beam
Horsepower:	1000

1901:	Built at McKie yard in East Boston for Boston and Bangor Steamship Co. to replace *Penobscot*
1901:	Boston and Bangor Steamship Co. became part of Eastern Steamship Co.
1901-1908:	Ran Boston-Bangor usually opposite similar *City of Bangor*
1909-1917:	Boston-Kennebec River
1918:	Boston-Bangor
1919-1923:	Boston-Kennebec River
1923:	September: ran aground near mouth of Kennebec River; declared a total loss; towed to Boston
1924:	Scrapped; remains burned

Cumberland (b. *Larchmont*)

Dimensions:	252.2x37x14.8
Tonnage:	Gross, 1605; Net, 896
Hull:	Wood
Engine:	Sidewheel, walking-beam
Horsepower:	1950

1885:	Built at New England Shipbuilding Co., Bath, Maine, for International Line
1885-1902:	International Line, Boston-Portland-Eastport-Lubec-Saint John, usually opposite sistership *State of Maine*
1902:	July: Sank in Boston Harbor after collision in fog with *Admiral Farragut*; sold to Joy Steamship Company; renamed *Larchmont*
1902-1907:	On Joy Line's low-fare overnight route, New York to Providence, Rhode Island, usually opposite sistership, *Edgemont* (a. *State of Maine*)
1907:	February 11: Rammed amidships by schooner *Harry Knowlton* off Watch Hill, Rhode Island, en route to New York at 11:40 P.M.; sank in twenty minutes; temperature ten degrees, seas rough; many died from escaping steam, many from extreme cold; only sixteen of 126 aboard survived; considered most serious steamship accident on Long Island Sound

Della Collins

Dimensions:	106.8x29.6x5.3
Tonnage:	Gross, 194; Net, 174
Hull:	Wood
Engine:	Sternwheel
Horsepower:	300

1879:	Built at McKie Shipyard, East Boston, for Kennebec Steamboat Company to meet the overnight steamer from Boston at Gardiner and carry transferred passengers and cargo to landings farther up Kennebec River as far as Augusta
1915:	Replaced by new *City of Augusta* and scrapped

Evangeline (b. *Yarmouth Castle*)

Dimensions:	365.5(378)x55x26.7
Tonnage:	Gross, 5043
Hull:	Steel
Engines:	Twin-screw single-reduction geared turbines
Horsepower:	7500

1927:	Built with sistership, *Yarmouth*, at William Cramp and Son Ship and Engine Co., Philadelphia
1927-1941:	Operated on various routes for Eastern Steamship Lines, mainly summers between Boston and Yarmouth, N.S., and winters on cruises out of New York to Bermuda or Nassau
1941:	On charter ordered by government to Alcoa Lines to run to bases in Bermuda, the Bahamas, and the Caribbean
1942-1946:	Troopship for U. S. Army in both Atlantic and Pacific
1946-1947:	Took one full year (February, 1946-February, 1947) to be rebuilt for peacetime service
1947:	Operated briefly on cruises by Eastern Steamship Lines,
1947-1954:	Expensive to operate with post-war costs; left idle in New York
1954:	Summer season on Boston-Yarmouth run after sistership, *Yarmouth*, had been sold
1954:	Sold for cruise services out of Miami
1954-1965:	Assigned to various short inexpensive cruises, mostly out of Miami to Nassau or nearby Caribbean ports
1964:	Name changed to *Yarmouth Castle*
1965:	Burned and sank en route Miami-Nassau

George Washington (b. *Gascogne*)

Dimensions:	375.5(390)x54x17.2 (Draft)
Tonnage:	Gross, 5184, Net, 3167
Hull:	Steel
Engine:	Single screw driven by two Curtis single-reduction geared turbines
Horsepower:	4750

1924:	Built with sistership, *Robert E. Lee*, for the Old Dominion Division (New York to Norfolk) of Eastern Steamship
1925-1931:	Summers on New York-Norfolk route
1925-1927:	Winters on New York-Jacksonville-Miami route of the Clyde Line under charter
1928-1931:	Winters on Eastern Steamship's New York-Boston route
1932-1941:	All year on Eastern's Old Dominion Division between New York and Norfolk
1942-1945:	Under charter mandated by government to Alcoa Lines to carry troops and supplies during Second World War for the most part out of New York to Bermuda or to the Caribbean
1945:	Sold by Eastern Steamship to War Shipping Administration, which continued charter to Alcoa
1946:	Released from military duties by the government
1946:	Operated by Alcoa in cruise service: New York-Bermuda
1948:	Sold to Alaska Transportation Co. of Seattle for cruise route Seattle-Alaska
1949:	Sold to Cie. Generale Transatlantique for service between France and French possessions in the Caribbean; renamed *Gascogne*
1950-1955:	Sold to Messageries Maritimes for a service between Marseilles and French Indo-China
1955:	Scrapped at Hong Kong

Governor Cobb (b. U.S.S. Cobb)

Dimensions:	289.1x54x18
Tonnage:	Gross, 2522; Net, 1556
Hull:	Steel
Engines:	Triple-screw direct-acting Parsons turbines
Horsepower:	4200

1906:	Built at Chester, Pennsylvaia, for Eastern Steamship's International Division. Engines by W. and A. Fletcher of Hoboken. First American steamer to be equipped with turbine engines
1906-1917:	Ran summers on Eastern Steamship's International route usually making the direct round trip between Boston and St. John; winters chartered to Peninsular and Occidental Line to run between Knight's Key or Key West and Havana
1918:	Chartered to government during First World War to serve as Merchant Marine training vessel
1920-1936:	Sold in 1920 to Peninsular and Occidental to serve on their route all year. Became a spare boat in 1931 after arrival of *Florida*
1936-1937:	Sold by P and O; served as day boat between Boston and Provincetown
1938-1942:	In lay-up
1942:	Converted for Coast Guard service in the Atlantic
1946:	In reserve fleet in James River, Virginia
1948:	Scrapped

Governor Dingley

Dimensions:	298.6(323)x60.8x17.8
Tonnage:	Gross, 3826; Net, 2856
Hull:	Steel
Engine:	Single-screw triple-expansion, reciprocating
Horsepower:	2500

1899:	Built at Chester, Pennsylvania, for the Portland Steam Packet Co. to replace lost *Portland*
1899-1909:	Ran overnight Boston-Portland opposite *Bay State*
1901:	Company purchased by Eastern Steamship
1910-1917:	International Line
1918:	On charter to Government during First World War as Merchant Marine training ship
1919-1931:	International Line
1934:	Scrapped

Hamilton

Dimensions:	Before 1913: 305.8x42x17
	After 1913: 351.8x42x17
Tonnage:	Before 1913: Gross, 3127, Net, 2025
	After 1913: Gross, 3723, Net, 2430
Hull:	Steel
Engine:	Single-screw, reciprocating
Horsepower:	3500

1899:	Built with sistership *Jefferson* at Chester, Pennsylvania, for Old Dominion Steamship Co.'s New York-Norfolk route
1913:	Lengthened about 45 feet
1923:	Company purchased by Eastern Steamship Lines, Inc.
1933:	Scrapped

Harvard

Dimensions:	376(407)x61x20.2(Draught)
Tonnage:	3818
Hull:	Steel
Engines:	Triple screw direct acting Parsons turbines
Horsepower:	10,000

1907:	Built at Chester, Pennsylvania, with sistership, *Yale*, for Metropolitan Line
1907-1910:	Operated on Metropolitan Line's New York-Boston overnight service
1910:	Sold with sistership, *Yale*, for a service on West Coast
1911-1917:	Operated opposite sistership, *Yale*, between San Francisco and Los Angeles; route later extended to San Diego
1917-1918:	Troopship in English Channel during First World War (temporarily renamed *Charles*)
1919-1931:	Returned to San Francisco-Los Angeles-San Diego run
1931:	May 30: Ran on rocks at Point Arguello when southbound; total loss

Herman Winter

Dimensions:	271.8x41.6x19.2
Tonnage:	Gross, 2625; Net, 1768
Hull:	Iron
Engine:	Single screw, reciprocating
Horsepower:	2000

1887:	Built at Philadelphia for Metropolitan Line
1887-1917:	Ran as cargo vessel on Metropolitan Line's New York-Boston route
1911:	Metropolitian Line absorbed by Eastern Steamship
1917:	Sold to U. S. government during First World War

H. F. Dimock

Dimensions:	271.8x41.6x19.2
Tonnage:	Gross, 2625; Net, 1786
Hull:	Iron
Engine:	Single screw, reciprocating
Horsepower:	2000

1884:	Built at Philadelphia as cargo vessel for Metropolitan Steamship Co.
1911:	Metropolitan Line absorbed by Eastern Steamship
1884-1917:	Ran on Metropolitan Line's New York-Boston route
1917:	Sold to U. S. government during First World War

H. M. Whitney

Dimensions: 271.8x43x19.2
Tonnage: Gross, 2706; Net, 1790
Hull: Iron
Engine: Single screw, reciprocating
Horsepower: 2800

1890:   Built at Philadelphia as cargo vessel for Metropolitan Steamship Co.
1890-1917:   Ran on Metropolitan Line's New York-Boston route
1911:   Metropolitan Line absorbed by Eastern Steamship
1917:   Sold to U. S. government during First World War

Jamestown

Dimensions: 299.5x40x16.8
Tonnage: Gross, 2898; Net, 2126
Hull: Steel
Engine: Single screw, reciprocating
Horsepower: 3197

1894:   Built at Chester, Pennsylvania, for the Old Dominion Steamship Company
1894-1911:   Ran New York-Norfolk for Old Dominion Line
1911-1925:   Spare ship for Old Dominion
1923:   Old Dominion purchased by Eastern Steamship Lines, Inc.
1925:   Scrapped

James S. Whitney

Dimensions: 278.5x43x29
Tonnage: Gross, 2707; Net, 1926
Hull: Steel
Engine: Single screw, reciprocating
Horsepower: 2600

1900:   Built at Wilmington, Delaware, as a cargo vessel for the Metropolitan Steamship Company
1911:   Metropolitan Line became part of Eastern Steamship
1900-1917:   Operated on New York-Boston route of Metropolitan Steamship Company
1917:   Sold to government during First World War

116

Jefferson

Dimensions:	Before 1913: 305.8x42x17
	After 1913: 351.8x42x17
Tonnage:	Before 1913: Gross, 3127, Net, 2025
	After 1913: Gross, 3723, Net, 2392
Hull:	Steel
Engine:	Single-screw, reciprocating
Horsepower:	3450

1899:	Built with sistership *Hamilton* at Chester, Pennsylvania, for Old Dominion Steamship Co.'s New York-Norfolk route
1913:	Lengthened about 45 feet
1923:	Company purchased by Eastern Steamship Lines, Inc.
1933:	Scrapped

J. T. Morse (b. *Yankee*)

Dimensions:	199(214)x31x12.1
Tonnage:	Gross, 780; Net, 410
Hull:	Wood
Engine:	Sidewheel, walking-beam
Horsepower:	600

1904:	Built in Boston for Eastern Steamship Company
1904-1931:	Ran summer season between Rockland and Bar Harbor, Maine, with stops along the way in Penobscot Bay; connected with Boston-Bangor boats at Rockland
1933:	Sold for excursion service in New York; renamed *Yankee*; freight deck opened for passengers
1933-1939:	Excursion service around New York; mostly Battery Park to Coney Island
1939-1941:	Laid up at Athens, New York
1941:	Scrapped

Kennebec (b. *Iroquois*)

Dimensions:	256x37.6x13.1
Tonnage:	Gross, 1652; Net, 1271
Hull:	Wood
Engine:	Sidewheel, walking-beam
Horsepower:	1400

1889:	Built at New England Shipbuilding Co., Bath, Maine, for Kennebec Steamship Company
1889-1905:	On seasonal route Boston-Kennebec River, usually opposite *Sagadahoc*
1901:	Kennebec Line became first line of Eastern Steamship Co.
1905:	Sold to Enterprise Steamship Co.
1905-1907:	On low-fare New York-Fall River, Massachusetts, overnight route of Enterprise Line
1907:	Sold to Joy Steamship Company
1910:	Sold to McAllister Brothers
1911-1915:	Chartered and later sold to Manhattan Navigation Co. for low-fare route between New York and Albany
1912:	Renamed *Iroquois*
1915-1917:	Laid up
1918:	Renamed *Iro*; carried supplies for U. S. Navy around port of Norfolk, Virginia
1919-1924:	Laid up in Elizabeth River, Virginia
1924:	Burned

Massachusetts (b. *Shawmut*, c. *Oglala*)

Dimensions:	375x52.2x30.2
Tonnage:	Gross, 4779; Net, 2575 (although not clear at which phase measurement taken)
Hull:	Steel
Engines:	Twin-screw reciprocating, triple expansion
Horsepower:	7000

1907:	Built at William Cramp and Son, Philadelphia, with sisterships *Bunker Hill* and *Old Colony* first as a freighter for the New England Steamship Company (subsidiary of New Haven Railroad) to compete on the the New York-Boston around-the-cape route aginst the Metropolitan Line's *Yale* and *Harvard*
1910-1911:	Passenger accommodations added and fuel changed to oil when New Haven RR decided to operate these ships on a passenger and cargo route New York-Boston, after Metropolitan sold *Yale* and *Harvard*
1911-1917:	Operated with sistership, *Bunker Hill*, on New York-Boston passenger and freight service for Eastern Steamship; passenger accommodations considerably increased in 1912
1917-1941:	In the U.S. Navy as Minelayer, U.S.S. *Shawmut*
1928:	Name changed to U.S.S. *Oglala*
1941:	Sunk during Japanese bombing of Pearl Harbor, subsequently raised and repaired
1941-1945:	Served in Pacific as a supply ship
1946:	Scrapped

Mineola

Dimensions:	121x26x9.6
Tonnage:	Gross, 295; Net, 107
Hull:	Wood
Engine:	Single screw
Horsepower:	450

1901:	Built at Port Clyde, Maine
1901-1917:	On Captain I. E. Archibald's Rockland-Portland route
1906:	Line sold to Eastern Steamship Co.
1919:	Sold to the Blackstone Navigation Co. of Pawtucket, Rhode Island; operated on both excursion and cargo runs in Narragansett Bay
1929:	Sank at Pawtucket; later raised, towed out to sea and sunk

Monhegan

Dimensions:	128x26.7x11.2
Tonnage:	Gross, 376; Net, 198
Hull:	Wood
Engine:	Single screw
Horsepower:	900

1903:	Built at Rockland for Capt. I. E. Archibald
1904-1917:	On Rockland-Portland route
1906:	Line purchased by Eastern Steamship Co.
1917:	Route given up
1918:	Ran Boston-Gloucester under charter
1925:	Sold by Eastern to Blackstone Valley Transportation Co.
1925-1938:	On various routes on Narragansett Bay, mainly Providence-Block Island
1938:	Badly damaged at pier in Providence during September, 1938, Hurricane
1939:	Towed to Prudence Island in Narragansett Bay to become a nightclub; never used; later scrapped

New York

Dimensions:	384.3(402)X50(72.5)X28
Tonnage:	Gross, 4989
Hull:	Steel
Engines:	Twin-screw geared turbines
Horsepower:	7600

1924:	Built with sistership, *Boston*, at Bethlehem Steel yard, Sparrows Point, Maryland
1924-1941:	Summer service, opposite *Boston* on Eastern Steamship's New York-Boston route
1942:	Barracks ship for Merchant Martine training school at Staten Island, New York
1942:	Aug: Strengthened, armed, and painted gray for assignment overseas
1942:	Sept. 23: Joined convoy of inland water vessels destined for Great Britain
1942:	Sept. 25: Torpedoed and sunk in Atlantic

North Land

Dimensions:	304(325)x47.2x19.8
Tonnage:	Gross, 3282; Net, 1973
Hull:	Steel
Engine:	Twin screw, reciprocating
Horsepower:	4000

1910:	Built for New York-Portland route of Maine Steamship Company (then a part of the Hartford and New York Transportation Co., which was in turn a subsidiary of the New Haven Railroad) to replace *Horatio Hall* lost off Cape Cod in 1909
1910-1917:	Ran New York-Portland usually opposite *North Star*
1911:	Maine Steamship Company became part of Eastern Steamship Corp.
1918:	Charter to U. S. government during First World War
1920-1923:	New York-Boston opposite *Calvin Austin*
1924-1926:	Boston-Yarmouth
1926-1931:	Summers, New York-Portland; winters, chartered to Peninsular and Occidental Line for service between Florida and Havana
1932:	Laid up, Boston
1933:	Scrapped

North Star

Dimensions:	298.8x40x17.2
Tonnage:	Gross, 3150; Net, 1999
Hull:	Steel
Engine:	Single screw, reciprocating
Horsepower:	4200

1901:	Built at Chester, Pennsylvania, for New York-Portland route of Maine Steamship Co. Similar to *John Englis* of 1896 (sold to government, 1898) and *Horatio Hall* (rammed by *H. F. Dimock* and sunk off Cape Cod, March, 1909)
1901-c.1914:	New York-Portland
c.1915-1919:	Boston-Yarmouth
1919:	Aground in fog, August 8, 1919; hull damaged; declared total loss

Old Colony

Dimensions:	375x52.2x30.2
Tonnage:	Gross, 4779; Net, 2428 (although not clear at which phase these measurements were taken)
Hull:	Steel
Engines:	Triple-screw direct-acting Parsons turbines
Horsepower:	5000

1907:	Built with sisterships, *Massachusetts* and *Bunker Hill*, at William Cramp and Son, Philadelphia, at first as freighter for Merchants Line (New York-Boston) of New England Steamship Company (subsidiary of New Haven Railroad)
1911:	Rebuilt with passenger accommodations added
1911-1918:	Ran on Maine Steamship Company's route between New York and Portland
1918:	Sold first to U. S. government for service in First World War; resold to French interests; wrecked and abandoned while in French service

Prince Arthur

Dimensions:	290x38x16.5
Tonnage:	Gross, 2040
Hull:	Steel
Engine:	Single screw, reciprocating

1899:	Built at Hull, England, for Canadian-owned Boston and Yarmouth Steamship Co., Ltd.
1899-1914:	Operated Boston-Yarmouth
1912:	Company purchased by Eastern Steamship Co.
1915-1919:	Served as Hospital Ship for British in European waters during First World War
1920-1926:	Boston-Yarmouth
1926-1928:	Often on International Line. Boston-St. John
1929:	Scrapped

Prince George

Dimensions:	290x38x16.5
Tonnage:	Gross, 2040
Hull:	Steel
Engine:	Single screw, reciprocating

1899:	Built at Hull, England, for Canadian-owned Boston and Yarmouth Steamship Co., Ltd.
1899-1914:	Operated Boston-Yarmouth
1912:	Company purchased by Eastern Steamship Co.
1915-1919:	Served as Hospital Ship for British in European waters during First World War
1920-1928:	Boston-Yarmouth
1929:	Scrapped

Ransom B. Fuller (b. Broadway)

Dimensions:	277.5x40.1x14 (1909: lenthened to 317.5')
Tonnage:	Before 1910: Gross, 1862; Net, 1023
	After 1910: Gross, 2329; Net, 1617
Hull:	Wood
Engine:	Sidewheel, walking-beam
Horsepower:	1600

1902:	Built by New England Shipbuilding Company, Bath, Maine
1902-1909:	On Kennebec Line of Eastern Steamship Co.
1909-1910:	Cut in two and forty-five feet added forward of stack to create greater passenger capacity
1910-1925:	Boston-Portland route
1925:	Sold to Charles Dimon; renamed *Broadway*, used only occasionally on excursion routes in New York harbor.
c.1930:	Used by Salvation Army as barracks for unemployed seamen at Staten Island
c.1935:	Partially scrapped at Newburgh, New York; hull towed to Cornwall, New York

Robert E. Lee

Dimensions:	375.5x54x17.2 (Draft)
Tonnage:	Gross, 5184
Hull:	Steel
Engine:	Twin screw geared turbines
Horsepower:	4750

1924:	Built with sistership, *George Washington*, for Old Dominion Division (New York to Norfolk) of Eastern Steamship Co.
1925-1931:	Summers on New York-Norfolk route
1925-1927:	Winters on New York-Jacksonville-Miami route of the Clyde Line under charter
1928-1931:	Winters on Eastern Steamship's New York-Boston route
1932-1941:	All year on Eastern's Old Dominion Division between New York and Norfolk
1942:	Under charter mandated by government to Alcoa Lines at first and then later sold to federal Maritime Commission but still chartered to Alcoa to carry troops and supplies during Second World War to Bermuda or to the Caribbean
1942:	Torpedoed and sunk in Gulf of Mexico by German U-Boat

Sagadaoc (a. *Star of the East*; c. *Greenport*)

Dimensions:	244.2x35.2x12.8
Tonnage:	Gross, 1413; Net, 1266
Hull:	Wood
Engine:	Sidewheel, walking-beam
Horsepower:	1000

1866:	Built as *Star of the East* for Kennebec Steamboat Co.
1866-1888:	Ran alone, ice-free months only, alternate nights between Boston and Gardiner, with landings along the Kennebec
1889:	Addition of new steamer *Kennebec* made daily service possible
1890:	Considerably rebuilt and renamed *Sagadahoc*
1890-1901:	Ran opposite *Kennebec* on Kennebec Line
1901:	Company became first line of Eastern Steamship Company
1902:	Replaced by new steamer *Ransom B. Fuller*; sold to Montauk Steamboat Co.; renamed *Greenport*
1907-1908:	Rerturned to Morse interests; operated on Morse's Citizen's Line (New York-Troy overnight) opposite much larger (but equally antique) *Dean Richmond* after that line lost both of its steamers, *City of Troy* and *Saratoga*, and until they were replaced by the new *Trojan* and *Rensselaer* in 1909
1912-1914:	Operated on a low-fare line New York-Albany overnight opposite *Fenimore* (a. *Frank Jones*) by the Hudson Navigation Co. in an effort to drive out the Manhattan Line, an independent low-fare line on the same route
c. 1915:	Scrapped, nearly fifty years old

St. Croix

Dimensions:	240.7x40.4x25.9
Tonnage:	Gross, 1993; Net, 1064
Hull:	Wood
Engine:	Single-screw, reciprocating
Horsepower:	2700

1895:	Built at Bath, Maine, for the International Steamship Co.
1895-1905:	Ran on direct route Boston-St. John
1901:	Company absorbed by Eastern Steamship
1905:	Sold to Enterprise Line to operate on a low-fare line between New York and Providence
1907:	Returned to Eastern Steamship in lieu of unpaid balance (which was probably most of it) when Enterprise went out of business
1908:	Sold to Northern Pacific Steamship Co. for a route between Seattle and Alaska
1909:	Chartered for a winter route between San Francisco and Los Angeles; burned at sea

Saint John (b. Antaeus)

Dimensions: 387.4(403)x61x22.5
Tonnage: Gross, 6175
Hull: Steel
Engine: Twin-screw geared turbines
Horsepower: 14,250

1931-1932:	Built at Newport News Shipbuilding and Dry Dock Co. with sistership, *Acadia*, for Eastern Steamship Lines
1932-1941:	Served on various routes for Eastern Steamship: mainly as a winter boat for its New York-Boston service and on summer routes from Boston to St. John, N.B. Also made between-season cruises from New York or Boston to Bermuda or Nassau.
1939:	Special trip to France to evacuate Americans from Europe at war..
1941:	Requisitioned by U. S. government for mandated charter to Alcoa Lines to operate between New Orleans and bases in the Caribbean; before charter started taken by government and converted to seaplane tender; renamed *Antaeus*
1943:	Converted to Hospital Ship and served mainly in the Pacific; details of service and ultimate disposition after the war not known

State of Maine (b. Edgemont, c. Cape May)

Dimensions: 241x37.1x14.6
Tonnage: Gross, 1409; Net, 818
Hull: Wood
Engine: Sidewheel, walking-beam
Horsepower: 1200

1882:	Built at New England Shipbuilding Co., Bath, Maine, for International Line
1882-1901:	International Line, Boston-Portland-Eastport-Lubec-Saint John usually opposite sistership *Cumberland* of 1885
1901-1903:	International Division of Eastern Steamship Co.
1904:	Sold to Joy Steamship Co., renamed *Edgemont*
1904-1915:	Joy Line's overnight route between New York and Providence, Rhode Island; after 1910 as spare
1915:	Sold for service Philadelphia-Cape May; renamed *Cape May*; ran only season of 1916
1916-1924:	Laid up in Philadelphia
1924:	Scrapped

Yale (b. Greyhound)

Dimensions:	376(407)x61x20.2(Draught)
Tonnage:	3818
Hull:	Steel
Engines:	Triple screw direct acting Parsons turbines
Horsepower:	10,000

1907:	Built at Chester, Pennsylvania, with sistership, *Harvard*, for Metropolitan Line
1907-1910:	Operated on Metropolitan Line's New York-Boston overnight service
1910:	Sold with sistership, *Harvard*, for a service on West Coast
1911-1917:	Operated opposite sistership, *Harvard*, between San Francisco and Los Angeles; route later extended to San Diego
1917-1918:	Troopship in English Channel during First World War
1919-1931:	Returned to San Francisco-Los Angeles-San Diego run
1931-1936:	Alone on the route after loss of *Harvard* in 1931
1936:	Route given up
1936-1942:	Laid up
1942-1946:	Barracks ship for Navy, renamed U. S. S. *Greyhound*
1949:	Scrapped

Yarmouth (b. Yarmouth Castle, c. Queen of Nassau, d. Yarmouth Castle, e. Yarmouth, f. Elizabeth A.)

Dimensions:	365.5(378)x55.7x26.7
Tonnage:	Gross, 5043
Hull:	Steel
Engine:	Twin-screw single-reduction geared turbines
Horsepower:	7500

1927:	Built with sistership, *Evangeline*, at William Cramp and Son Ship and Engine Co., Philadelphia
1927-1941:	Operated on various routes for Eastern Steamship Lines, mainly summers between Boston and Yarmouth, N.S., and winters on cruises out of New York to Bermuda or Nassau
1941:	On charter ordered by government to Alcoa Lines to run between New Orleans and bases in the Caribbean
1942-1946:	Troopship for U. S. Army in both Atlantic and Pacific
1946-1947:	Took one full year (February, 1946-February, 1947) to be rebuilt for peacetime service
1947-1954:	Operated by Eastern Steamship Lines Boston-Yarmouth in summer and cruises, mostly out of New York, in winter
1954:	Sold for cruise services out of Miami; name changed to *Yarmouth Castle*; registered in Panama
1954-1956:	Ran under contract to government of Nassau on regular twice-a-week round trips between Miami and Nassau, renamed *Queen of Nassau*
1956:	Name restored to *Yarmouth Castle*
1956-1966:	Operated by various companies on various cruise routes but primarily on short inexpensive cruises out of Miami
1964:	Name restored to *Yarmouth*
1966:	Sold to Greek owners for Mediterranean cruise service and renamed *Elizabeth A*. Never operated by new owners; placed in lay-up at Elefsis and later scrapped

Index